THE

HALF

MILLIONAIRE
REAL ESTATE AGENT

THE

HALF

MILLIONAIRE

REAL ESTATE AGENT

THE 52 SECRETS TO MAKING A HALF
MILLION DOLLARS A YEAR WHILE
WORKING A 20-HOUR WORK WEEK

BRIAN ERNST

ISBN-13: 978-1-950710-07-2 (Amazon print)
ISBN-13: 978-1-950710-08-9 (Ingram Spark) Paperback
ISBN-13: 978-1-950710-09-6 (Ingram Spark) Hardcover
ISBN-13: 978-1-950710-10-2 (Smashwords)

For bulk purchase and for booking, contact:

Brian Ernst
brian@brianernst.net

2970 Peachtree Circle
Aurora, IL 60502
(630) 730-0838

Acknowledgements

My mom, Celeste Jacklin, for all of her support throughout the years with my ups and downs in my real estate career and her unconditional love, without which I would not be as successful as I am today. Mom was also an integral part of helping me get the systems in place for the mailers and magnets that I've used throughout my career. These have been the backbone of my business. Thanks, mom!

My dad, Rick Ernst, for having a business when I was younger where he needed those mailers sent out. It's where my mom learned how to do it so efficiently! I learned as a child that these mailers were a very important thing to use to stay in front of people. Dad taught me that half of life is showing up, and the other half is what you do when you show up. This book is a reflection of that.

My team member, Nikki Criel, for whatever it is that she wants to be thanked for at this moment—there are just too many things to list!

My team member, Jon Plude, for immediately and unrelentingly doing the work and showing how quickly the secrets can have a huge effect in a very short period of time.

JoAnna Blackstock, for helping me start this project years ago and inspiring me to reach out to help others to take my business to a whole new level.

Everett O'Keefe, at Ignite Press for taking this book that I have been tinkering with for five years and finally getting it done in only a matter of months! His guidance and persistence in keeping me on track was very much needed and appreciated.

Dedication

I dedicate this book to my team members and coaching members throughout the years who proved to me that these secrets work, not just for me, but for other people too! By teaching these secrets to others, it helped me to better learn and refine the material in this book. It also reminded me what I needed to know when I restarted my career. I appreciate all of these people who helped me to remember that it's also about the journey and not just about the destination!

Table of Contents

Brian Ernst

Introduction

Welcome to the "grand illusion" of real estate: all the time, money, and freedom that you could ever have imagined! Well, at least that was the lie that I was fed when I first got into real estate. What I really found out is that we were either working or available for work seven days a week, every waking hour of the day. I recall taking phone calls and responding to questions or emails at 2:00 a.m. So, add up those hours.

What I'd like to share with you in this course is how to NOT work that many hours and find the success, find the time, find the freedom, and find the money that you want in real estate. In this course, you're going to learn the secrets to working a 20-hour work week while making $500,000 a year. I'm so excited to share these secrets with you so that you have the time, freedom, and flexibility of life that you really want to have.

*   *   *

Want to discuss putting the 52 Secrets to work for you?
Schedule a complimentary consultation through my website at
www.brianernstcoaching.com. I would love to discuss your
options with you personally.

The Real Estate Emergency

There is NO SUCH THING as a real estate emergency. I know that might sound funny to some people, but there really is no such thing as a real estate emergency. If there were, each real estate agent would provide the message, "If this is a real estate emergency, please hang up and dial 911," before connecting the caller to the agent. As far as I know, that does not happen.

This business can trick you into believing everything is an emergency. Real estate is so unlike other businesses in that there's no one standard across the board. Especially if you're on your own, there's no one telling you when you should start work and when you should go home. No one's clocking you out, so you have to remember to make it a priority to manage your time effectively and in a manner that will work for both you AND your client. If you stick to a schedule that works for you, you will find that many "emergencies" are, in fact, just problems that can be resolved in the morning. Remember, just because somebody else thinks something is an emergency doesn't mean it actually is. So, set your own schedule and stick to it!

Back in my first year in real estate, I remember a seller calling me in the middle of the night around 1:00 a.m. I was just starting out, so I didn't think twice about answering, believing it must be important. Turns out, they were locked out of their house, and I was expected to take care of it. Somehow, it was my fault even though they were the one who forgot their keys. Fortunately, I was able to ascertain enough information to figure out they could get into the house through the garage, and I could go back to sleep. Though the situation wasn't ideal for them, it certainly wasn't my problem, and I shouldn't have been expected to answer the phone at such a late hour. I shouldn't have to be available 24 hours a day, and neither should you.

In real estate, scenarios like the one I described are a common occurrence. It is unsustainable to set up unrealistic expectations such as 24 hours of availability. Sure, some days, you might be available at all hours for an "emergency," but the fact is, most days, you won't, and more importantly, you shouldn't have to be. My job as a real estate agent is to market, advise, and sell. Simple, yet full of complicated facets. To maintain my sanity, I had to learn to set boundaries for myself. These specific boundaries may not work for everyone, but they can be a good starting point for when you decide to set your own work-life balance boundaries. So, the first thing I did was to turn off my phone at 6:00 p.m. every night. I figured anyone who called after 6:00 p.m. could wait until morning. What I noticed was that by 9:00 a.m., most of the problems had resolved themselves.

Looking back, I can't recall any instance where I lost business because I wasn't available after 6:00 p.m. I know it can be a tough concept to embrace, and you're probably thinking to yourself, "Well, that might work for him, but I could never turn off my phone and get away with it." Trust me, there isn't a decent real estate agent out there who isn't thinking the same thing. But you definitely can, especially if you are consistent and set the expectations early. I added a disclaimer to my voicemail outgoing message that stated, "If this call is after business hours, your call will be returned the next business day." My clients then knew when to expect to hear back from me and understood that I wasn't ignoring them. The other thing I did was get a second personal phone that I used exclusively for friends and family. That way, I didn't have to worry that I was going to miss an important phone call from a family member when I turned my work phone off at 6:00 p.m.

Now, this only worked because I first set the expectations with my client, then followed through. So, if I did get any voicemails during my off-hours, I made sure the next morning to listen to them and prepare the necessary information for the return call. I made sure I checked back in with them and didn't waste their time (or mine) by not being prepared.

By doing this, you get your time back, your profit per hour goes up, and you're more prepared that next day to handle your client or potential client's needs. It is CRITICAL that you are prepared. The clients can sense it, so being prepared will not only make you feel more confident in the work you are doing, but it will make your clients more confident in you as well! It will help you build trust. When you take time for yourself in your off-hours, you're able to be more present and ready for your client during business hours.

I know for some, it is hard to find the motivation and keep the momentum going when you restrict yourself to working only during certain hours. As you probably know, the real estate business is fast-paced, and you want to keep the ball rolling; you don't want to feel like you've missed a big opportunity, so you have to make strides every day to continue to grow your business. But continuing momentum for your business does not mean you have to continue working 24/7. The advice I gave one coaching client who struggled with this was to take some time to help other real estate agents, especially those just starting out. When you give advice to someone or you help them through an issue, it is much harder to ignore that advice that you've given out because no one wants to feel like a hypocrite. You are then able to keep your schedule to manageable hours but also feel like you have that extra layer of accountability to keep the momentum building for your business.

The advice I gave that coaching client is only one way to keep the motivation going day in and out by forcing yourself to stop work at the sound of the proverbial bell every night. But there are other things you can do to keep the momentum going and enjoy a life outside of your work—you just have to work hard to find what works for you. You'll likely find that a more structured approach to your day will actually help you in the long run, as it helps you keep that consistency. Momentum is built on continued progress. As long as you keep moving forward, prioritizing your work, and taking each task one at a time instead of putting out the fire for whoever is screaming the loudest, you won't lose that momentum. Just remember, there's NO SUCH THING as a real estate emergency, so don't let someone else's sense of urgency dictate how you handle your business.

Tools for Saving Time

Are you aware of all the cheap and/or free time-saving tools that are available to you today? One of the best things about being in real estate in today's world is the technology that is available to you, literally at your fingertips. My biggest focus for managing work is making sure I have my days scheduled out and organized. When I started in the business, I used an at-a-glance day planner, complete with a list of things to do in it. Problem was, if I didn't have my planner with me, I couldn't schedule an appointment, and I couldn't confirm appointments on the physical paper calendar. Eventually, I switched over to using a digital calendar.

I converted all my hand-written and organized appointments and reminders into a Google Calendar that I could then share with clients. I could move appointments around without having to use white-out, and the changes were reflected automatically on all my digital platforms like my phone, computer, and tablet. Some of you may already use Google Calendars, but I like to include it in my list of time saving tools anyway. Sometimes, the more obvious tools are the ones that are most overlooked, especially if you aren't using all the features the calendar has to offer. For example, Google Calendars allows every guest you invite to an event to confirm the appointment.

Another helpful tool to make sure you have in your arsenal is any type of online signature platform. Tradition tells us that we should be meeting our clients—either having them meet us at our office, their home, or some other location—then getting the physical signatures that will then be shared with the sellers/buyers. Basically, we want everyone involved spend their precious time getting documents signed in person, on paper. But, as comforting it may be to physically sign a document, most clients will gladly save their time and energy to virtually sign a document and get it to you in a way that can accommodate their busy schedules.

Instead, you can send your paperwork through Dotloop, DocuSign, or any other type of digital signature program and get the documents to your clients as soon as possible. Make sure you familiarize yourself with the program before you send out your first time-sensitive document. Most programs are fairly straightforward and user-friendly, but it never hurts to take a few extra minutes to browse their "how-to" sections to get comfortable with what you are doing. Once I became a virtual signature pro, it saved me and my clients time and allowed me to get to the point where I didn't even need to physically go to listing appointments because I just sent my clients the documents virtually. Once they received the documents, they were able to sign them and send them right back, allowing me to get moving onto my next tasks in a matter of minutes.

It is not in my (or your) best interest to work on non-"dollar productive" activities. Setting up a showing appointment doesn't make me any money directly. It needs to happen, but it's not getting me a new listing. To save time, I now use a showing desk. It took me a while to understand the importance of this tool, and I spent about half my career either having appointments set up directly through the MLS or through the seller. If you think about it, it's probably not in your best interest to have another agent talking directly to your seller.

ShowingTime is one of the many automated services that can be set up to allow the seller to directly confirm and reschedule showing requests. I can easily block out times and days when the property is unavailable to show. I can have a live person confirm with a phone call, there are automatic emails and texts, and the system sends out requests for feedback multiple times. ShowingTime provides me with the options to change the content and frequency of the feedback requests and customize the verbal and non-verbal communication with my clients so it is on-brand and doesn't sound like it is coming from a third party.

When I first signed up for a showing desk program, I probably saved three to four hours a week, if not more, from not having to chase people down to get their appointments scheduled. The mental energy I saved alone was worth the price of admission. The stress of not being able to get ahold of the seller, set up an appointment, or deal with the seller constantly asking for feedback is simply eliminated. It really is a wonderful time saver, and the money spent is more than made up for in the time I saved by using their services.

One last tool I'll mention is a visual voicemail tool, such as YouMail or the Google Voice service. Each phone carrier usually has a version of it as well, which is what I use. These services translate the voice message into text form and email it to you. This way, I'm able to quickly read the voicemail message and get the gist of the call without actually having to listen to it. It also makes it easier to keep track of important details left in a voicemail, as I don't have to try to write down the information while listening or listen to it ten times to make sure I got it all. The information is all there in text form for me to reference later, if needed. I can get through my messages much quicker, thus enabling me to reply that much quicker as well.

Using cheap or free time-saving tools can easily add 10 hours back to your week. This will increase your productivity and provide you with more time to build client relationships or simply take a longer lunch break (or actually HAVE the time to take a lunch break!). Don't forget that these tools are out there and that they exist to help you make your life easier. Don't be afraid to invest the time upfront to try them, especially the free ones (though, often, paid-for tools have a free trial period), and see how you can best optimize your time and effort.

Secret 3

Secret Agent

Don't be a secret agent! That might sound funny—we're talking real estate, not government agencies. You don't want to be doing real estate so quietly that you never get new business because NO ONE KNOWS that you're in the industry. What I'm about to tell you with this secret, most people will resist. Many of the real estate agents I talk to don't do and don't want to do these things.

The first step to ensure that you don't act like a secret agent is to actually let people know that you're in real estate. A good way to do this is to use your car. I started with sign magnets on the side of my car, but that's not all there is. You can use decals on the back of windows and license plate frames, and people even have their cars wrapped entirely with an advertisement. Don't forget about personalized license plates!

I can't tell you how many times this has come up when I'm coaching or training real estate agents. People are scared to use any form of car advertisement because they are afraid it's too tacky. They're afraid it's gaudy. I've heard, "Oh, my gosh. I'm not going to do that to my car. Oh, my gosh." The number of real estate conversions they'd have just because of the advertisements on their car would lead to enough deals to enable them to buy a separate car!

But believe me, it's not tacky, and it's not gaudy. When people see me driving around, going through different neighborhoods, they think, "Hey, there's Brian again. He's working a lot. Wow, he's working odd hours."

Reality is, I'm not always working. I'm just driving my car, but they don't know that, and that's what's important! They just see me and see my branding, and the next time they are on the hunt for a real estate agent, guess whose name comes up first? The one that is at the forefront of their mind: MINE!

It also has acted as an ice breaker for people to come up and talk to me about real estate. Visibility matters. For instance, if you're doing an open house, the potential buyers all see your car; they know where you are, and they know who you are. If you're parked in front of a new listing, they'll see you setting up the signs. From there, it's a small jump to, "That must be Brian over there. Hey, I want to go talk to him."

Don't be afraid to park your car in your driveway. It's a free billboard in your driveway. Seriously, what's better than that? So, go ahead, use your car as mobile advertisement; it can really help improve your visibility and get your name out there wherever you go.

The next thing I think is important to avoid being a secret agent that some people can be uncomfortable with is wearing your name tag. Oh, I know. I've heard it: "I never want to wear a name tag."

But I can't tell you how many times just wearing a name tag has led to someone asking me, "So, how's the market doing right now?" That's a lead! They just offered to engage you in a real estate conversation that would never have started had you not worn your name tag! Even if you're at the grocery store, at church, running errands, or wherever you go, having that name tag on will encourage conversations about real estate with people you might never had reached without it. It truly is amazing how many conversations you can engage in when you're not a secret agent, but it make take stepping out of your comfort zone.

Through the years, I've heard all the reasons why someone might be uncomfortable with putting themselves out there, but when they do take that step out, the money that results helps assuage their concerns. Some people, however, have to ask themselves, "Am I proud of what I do? Am I willing to take the steps necessary to succeed, even if it means moving out of my comfort zone?" If not, then get out of real estate! Don't do this! Pick a different career! The job isn't going to change; this is what it is. Embrace it!

People have often said to me, "Brian, I see you everywhere." I think to myself, "You see me everywhere? I haven't even been in this store before!" I could be freaked out by the statement, but instead, I embrace it. The more avenues there are where I am putting myself out there, the higher the likelihood that someone is going to see me and recognize me, and the higher the chance is that I will be able to turn that recognition into a sale.

Potential clients have seen my car. They've seen my signs. They've seen other marketing materials out there with my face on it. Part of my marketing strategy is to get potential clients to see me in at least three different spots consistently every single month. It's awesome stuff. If you want the business, you have to let people know. It's a really easy decision. Don't be a secret agent!

Let me finish this secret with a few examples. A few years ago, I was a manager at RE/MAX, and I was running a coaching group. I was explaining what a secret agent is, why you don't want to be one, and the steps you can take to avoid it, including name tags, branded merchandise, and signs and posters. One of the agents in the group— we'll call her Negative Nelly, or Nelly for short—was quite vocal and a bit obnoxious in her resistance to the ideas I was presenting. Her reasoning was that she'd be embarrassed to have her car branded where people could see it.

My first thought was, "Are you not proud of what you do for a living?" Then, as incredulity seeped in, "Are you embarrassed, or would you like to make an extra 10 grand a year? How is branding your car with something you're proud of embarrassing? When you graduate from college, are you embarrassed to put up your university alumni license plate frame? Heck no! You're proud. You're excited. That's how it should be with your real estate business." But no argument was going to change Nelly's mind.

Finally, it got to the point where we had the door magnets made for each broker's car knowing they weren't going to do it themselves. Everybody put theirs on and took pictures of their newly branded vehicles. Nelly then gave in and begrudgingly put hers on her car.

A week later, at the next meeting, Nelly came in with a big smile on her face. I'll admit, I was a little surprised that our resident Negative Nelly was giving off a positive vibe. So, I asked her, "Alright, what's going on?"

She said, "That day I left with the car magnets on, I went to show some houses, and one of the neighbors came up and approached me in between showing appointments because they noticed the magnets on my car, advertising me as a real estate agent. They had some questions about the property that was listed." Nelly went on to tell me this couple didn't have an agent, and after getting her contact info, they eventually became her clients!

In one week, her attitude and business had changed. She didn't even mean for it to happen. Nelly had put the magnets on her car because everyone else was doing it, but she probably left it on because she forgot or was too lazy to take them off. However, it did end up making a difference!

Now, does that happen all the time? Absolutely not. Sometimes, it takes a while for you to see an increase in business, but that doesn't mean it won't work.

I once told an agent to wear her name tag everywhere she went. She asked, "Everywhere? Even to the gym?"

"Yeah, do that." I wasn't sure she was going to take it that far, but I figured it couldn't hurt.

Turns out, she did wear her name tag everywhere, including the gym. And do you know what happened? She got an extra two deals that year, just from wearing her name tag to the gym!

Yeah. Let that sink in.

She could have been too embarrassed to be seen wearing a name tag to the gym, but even if she was embarrassed, her willingness to succeed outweighed that insecurity, and she benefitted from reaching out of her comfort zone.

The way I see it, these types of advertisements are easy and pretty low-cost ways to get your name out there. You're already driving your car around, and you're already walking around—why not advertise while you do it? Car magnets and name tags cost close to nothing. So, if you don't see a return on the investment right away, you're not out a huge chunk of change. You simply have to ask yourself, what is it worth to you to succeed?

* * *

If you would like to schedule a complimentary consultation, please visit my website at www.brianernstcoaching.com.

What Is Your Time Worth?

How much is your time worth? Let's do the math and think about this.

First, how much money did you make last year in real estate? I'm not talking about how much gross or how much you made in commissions. I'm talking about the actual money still sitting in your bank account after all your expenses.

Next, how many weeks did you work throughout the year? We know there are 52 weeks in a year, but did you really work 52 weeks? Most agents don't work 52 weeks.

Finally, how many hours did you work each week?

Alright, now divide last year's net income by the number of weeks you worked. Then divide that number by the amount of hours in the week you worked. THAT is what your time is worth!

(Net Income÷Number of weeks worked)÷Number of hours worked
= What your time is worth

For example, if you net $50,000 and worked 50 weeks at 30 hours a week:

$$(\$50,000 \div 50) \div 30 = \$32$$
You are worth $32 an hour!

I think it is crucial to actually take the time to sit down and literally do the math. It is so important to know what you are worth. Why? Let me tell you.

First, are you doing activities each day that aren't worth your time? For example, are you scrubbing your toilet? Cutting your lawn? Are you shoveling your own driveway? (That may not come up for many of you residing in warmer climates, but it does for me as I'm in Illinois.) If you think you can't afford to pay somebody to do something, the worth of your time comes into play. Your time is worth something every day, so you need to figure out which hours are "work."

When you go to hire other personnel, whether an admin or a transaction coordinator, it is so important that you know how much your time is worth and how much it is worth to you to hire someone else to do different aspects of the job. When you realize what you're making per hour and divide that out as opposed to what you have paid somebody else to do those tasks, you will know when it makes sense to hire somebody else. Once you've got the numbers in front of you, you can make the decision and feel confident that it is the right decision for where you are currently at in your real estate career.

The crucial component of knowing what your time is worth is important so you can focus more of your time and effort on your business and not let busy work distract you. You can pay someone else to do the more tedious activities, just as long as you are spending the extra time building your business and not sitting on the couch and watching Netflix. Remember that being busy and being productive are two different things.

I'll conclude this secret with a story about a real estate agent I once coached. We'll call him Oliver, Oliver the Overworked. When Oliver first came to me, he was killing himself, working long hours every day of the week. He worked primarily with these investors with very inexpensive, difficult properties that were short sales or foreclosures. We're talking 30 grand, 40 grand list price properties, VERY inexpensive. Many of them were condominiums, which meant they had mountains of paperwork associated with each sale because there were so many interested people even as they were going into foreclosure. And the short sales took FOREVER to get approval, IF they even got it.

So, Oliver's was working his rear off for these small listings, and he was making somewhere between 30 and 40 grand a year, killing himself. He had actually made more in the previous year because he had a higher price point. Now, he was working so often with such a cheap price point that he was putting in the time but not reaping the rewards. I am not just saying, "Don't go for a cheap price point." The key is to make sure everything is set up properly from the beginning.

Oliver was just setting up deals and making them happen, but he wasn't really thinking; he was just responding. He was paying for leads to come in versus understanding what those leads were and what the long-term benefits or drawbacks were. You may be thinking that you that you need to grow business, and just like Oliver, you may be growing it, but you won't be growing it in a sustainable way. You need to think about the longevity of your business and your business practices because if you aren't, you're going to be out of business.

So, here's how I helped Oliver. First, I focused on helping him restructure his focus to target a specific area instead of simply taking whatever came across his desk. I got him off the cheap, cheap, difficult deals on the buying side, and I had him focus much more on the listing side of things. What I didn't do was have him cut his hours. Instead, I got him listing properties that were more expensive, though reasonably priced. I had him target properties that were going for over $200,000. That's a HUGE difference in income right there in commission and other processes.

And this was the point where Oliver really started to see what his time was worth.

Before, it had been a bit of a hard sell to get him to change up how he was doing business, but once I broke it down for him, the lightbulb turned on. I said, "You're working these many hours for this much money. Broken down to an hourly rate, you're not even making minimum wage!" The numbers, when you look at them cold and unfeeling, can tell you quite a story. I mean, when someone's working as hard as he was, you have to convince yourself it's all worth it and you're making good money. Otherwise, why do it? But when you're looking at those numbers in plain black and white, it can be pretty shocking.

Because Oliver didn't understand what his time was worth, he didn't see the problems with the way he was doing business. Busy does not equal productive or lucrative. I can't tell you how many agents I know who are busy but not productive.

Brian Ernst

"I'm busy."

"Yes, but are you productive? Are you..."

"I'm busy." So that's a no, you're not productive.

If you don't know what your time is worth, you may not realize just how unproductive you are being with your valuable time. When Oliver changed his focus from the buyer's side to the selling side and invested that same money he was putting into buyer leads to instead get seller leads, it transformed his business!

It's not something that happens overnight. Once Oliver understood what he was worth and started to make strides toward using his time more effectively for his business, he was making well over $300,000 within a few years. So, now he was making more, but he still hadn't fully grasped the idea and hadn't learned to fully leverage his time. Oliver would tell me, "I don't want to pay somebody to do this when I can just do it myself."

I said, "Let's do the math again. How much are you making right now? Let's break it down to what you're getting paid per hour. Now, you're worth THIS much an hour. It's a heck of a lot more than when you were not even making minimum wage before. If you go do this activity, this is a $10 to $15 an hour job, and you're getting paid way more than that to do this. So, wouldn't it be easier to just leverage your time with somebody else doing those activities, and you can do whatever you want to do? Maybe hang out with your kids?"

Oliver's big into collecting cars, so I said, "Go drive your cars!" He also plays in a band, so I encouraged him to go do those fun things. Once he did, he realized he didn't want to go back! Oliver learned how to leverage his time efficiently and for the betterment of his business and his life outside of real estate.

So, find out what your time is worth and if what you're doing is worth your time. Do the math!

Terminology

There is a wide range of different terminology used in real estate. I'm going to call it old terminology versus new terminology, not-as-good practices and best practices for terminology. Why am I bringing this up? Because it has been an issue for me in the past when I think I'm communicating one idea to a client and they think I'm communicating something completely different. And it's cost me deals. If you can't communicate properly with your client, it's going to hurt your business.

Many of the times this came up during listing appointments when I was trying to describe to the client what their house was worth and why it was worth that much. One of those words is "comps." What's a comp? Not everybody's familiar with that terminology, and often, people are going to say, "What the heck are you talking about?"

If you use abbreviations and acronyms, it's important to assume the general public will not understand. They don't use these terms every day like we do. The client may just nod his or her head and smile and not let on that they are confused. So, just assume they don't know and use other words or phrases that they can understand to avoid the confusion altogether. For example, instead of "comp," use *relevant properties*. During a listing appointment, show them the relevant properties to their property.

Speaking of listing appointments, would you prefer to go on a listing appointment or a marketing consultation? What terminology do you think will appeal more to your clients? The terminology you use can change the dynamic of the situation and can help you put a positive spin on negative features of the listing. This is important when you're showing a property. How do you put a positive spin on road noise? It's *urban surf*.

Okay, maybe that's funny to some people, but it can work! Even though it may be a funny phrase, simply the fact that you, as the real estate agent, aren't focusing on the negative can help sell the house that much quicker.

Another piece of terminology that comes up often in real estate sales is "divorce." Just that simple word can be pretty polarizing, so I recommend you change it to *marital transition*. There is less of a stigma associated with that phrase, and hopefully, you won't turn off a buyer just because the word "divorce" triggers a subconscious negative response. And that's what I'm trying to get at. Words and phrases can have a big impact on your ability to sell a listing, so it is critical that you use language that doesn't confuse or alienate your clients or potential buyers.

Now, there are some changes in the real estate world that also need to be addressed. You have the old-school terminology that, in today's market, doesn't always convey the message or attitude you want and can turn off potential buyers and clients. One piece of terminology I want you to think about replacing is "commission." Instead, you should be referring to it as the *professional service fee*. Another is "listing presentation." Try *marketing consultation* instead. "Sales" or "closed transaction" should be replaced with *real buyers*. And lastly, "agent" can be replaced by *real estate professional*. Which sounds better to you? Do you see how each piece of new terminology puts a different spin and a different connotation with the word or phrase?

The terminology you use can have a big impact on how you are perceived and, by extension, how your business and associated listings are perceived.

Don't Go to the Office

DO NOT go in the office. Have your office in your home. Now, some people may say, "That doesn't work for me. I can't do that." And I do understand that there are situations where the distractions at home outweigh the benefits of having a home office—it can be hard to get work done in some cases. But I think you really need to look at all the benefits that are available to you when you have a home office.

When I first got into real estate, I realized the people who were selling the most houses, who were making the most money, were never in the office because they were actually out selling houses and making money. Those of us in the office weren't making any money because we weren't with clients! Most of the work done in the office ended up just helping *other* agents' listings and didn't actually help me make any money. So, why would you want to be in the office? Why would I drive a half an hour to an office and a half an hour back? That's an hour of my day that's gone. I could have used that selling houses, prospecting, and negotiating deals. Are there leads in the office? For the most part, I found the answer to be no.

The idea of going to the office has changed drastically from 20 or 30 years ago. It used to be that when someone was looking to find a house, they would go to a real estate office and talk to an agent. At that point, you had agents going into the office just to check their voicemail because they didn't have a business line at home, much less a cell phone to take the call on. Then, once technology was more of a factor, agents had to go into the office just to use the computer because it wasn't common practice for everyone to have a computer at home, much less a smartphone. So, though technology was on the rise, there was still a lot of business that depended on the phone and office landlines. This was something I faced early on in my career. We would have assigned floor time when we sat in the office waiting for the phone to ring. An interested client would call the office number and whoever was on the floor at the time would help that client out. This process works for the brokerage because they're getting clients to agents more quickly, but if it was my ad and my listing and I wasn't in the office at the time the client called, I would lose it, which never seemed fair to me.

Fortunately, that really isn't how it is done anymore. Technology has really changed how clients and buyers find and view real estate. Clients don't physically go into an office anymore, and agents are rarely forced to put the brokerage's number in any sort of prominence over their own. Most everything is done online or via the agent's cell phone. Right now, I'm with eXp Realty, and I don't actually have a physical office! It's a cloud-based brokerage, so everything is done virtually. So, I work out of my home office when I need to get work done, but that's it.

Some people say they want to work in an office outside of their home to escape their kids, or the barking dogs, etc. I get that. But realize that you can escape the craziness at home if you commit to it. Create a space for your home office that allows you to block out the sound of the rest of the house. Have a sign on the door that lets your family know, unless someone is bleeding or dying, you are not to be disturbed. Then, the hardest part is enforcing that. Don't wander out for a quick snack then get roped into taking the dog for a walk, for example. Set up the expectations ahead of time and let your family know, "Hey, these are the hours when I'm working. Pretend I'm not even here and only call me if it's something you'd call me about if I had an office in an office building." If you can set those expectations from the beginning, you will have no problem being productive in your home office.

Sometimes, it takes extreme measures, like setting down these types of rules with your family. If they're not supportive of that and you truly aren't able to work from home, there may be some larger issues at play. Having a supportive family and a support system you can lean on is crucial for having a successful business. But that's something we'll go into in more depth later in the book.

If you're still not sold on leaving the traditional office space, let me put it to you in terms of time spent during your day. (Remember, we now know what your time is worth!) So, you drive a half-hour to the office, get prepared for an appointment, drive a half-hour to the appointment, then another half-hour back to the office to hand the paperwork in or whatever else you need to do, and then go back home. How many hours of your day were wasted because you were on the road? Then there's all the time wasted once you're in the office. Too often, people will waste time chatting with coworkers or engaging in other frivolous distractions that might FEEL like they're work but really aren't.

There is simply no reason to go into the office. If you work for a company that has a central office and it requires you to attend an in-person training, sure, but other than that, what else is there but distractions?

You need to meet a client? Meet them at their property—it's the object of your relationship, after all, so it only makes sense.

You need to meet a buyer? Meet them at a coffee shop. It's easy, convenient, and you likely won't run into a coworker who wants to chat and take precious time away from your productivity.

Don't go into the office just for the sake of going in.

If you work for a brokerage that requires it, start looking elsewhere. It just doesn't make sense. Insist on working from home, and see how much your business grows when you're spending more time actually being productive. Time is money, and you're worth it to make sure your time is well-spent.

The Right Broker

Understand this: The real estate business, as it's been run over the course of my career so far, is rigged for failure. The success rates of agents, or lack thereof, is all the proof you need. Seven out of 10 agents quit in the first twelve months. There is also a large percent of agents that may not have dropped out, but they haven't done anything either. Last year (2018), in my board of realtors alone, 71% of the 18,000 agents did zero or one deal. It's appalling! Now, think about it more broadly. There are around 1.3 million realtors in the United States. I'm not talking about simply licensed agents but dues-paying, board-participating, MLS-accessing members. These are realtors who are literally PAYING to be real estate agents. And yet, only 3.3% did 25 deals or more. That breaks down to barely two deals a month. That's just insane!

Now, why is this the state of realty? Because these agents haven't yet grasped the fact that THEY ARE RUNNING A REAL ESTATE BUSINESS. So, how can you be successful running a real estate business? We've already gone over a few of the secrets to success, but this next one is one your broker may want you to shy away from.

Are you with the right broker? The topic of the right broker is huge and not discussed NEARLY enough at the level that I think it should be discussed at. The right broker is so important because the brokerage can either support you in building a successful business or can bring you down. So, let's get into it.

What are you getting from your brokerage, and what is it getting from you?

What is the commission split it is offering? There's no one standard across the board; different brokers will have varying commission splits. So, make sure you know what they're offering. You need to do the math. A high commission split on a larger volume of transactions doesn't necessarily make sense for the broker because the broker has to do more work. Remember, the brokerage is in this to make money. In some brokerages, including many of the larger companies, there is a cap to the amount of commission or fees you pay per year. Once you hit that cap, you get 100% of your commission. My past two companies have been exactly like that. Once that cap is reached, you may have a few small transaction fees, but you're now raking in the bulk of the cash. After a certain number of transactions, your cap is reached, and the broker no longer makes any money off of you—it's now losing it.

So, in these cases, it doesn't make financial sense for the brokerage to encourage you or support you to produce at such a high level. Some offices have different rules for the agents who actually do cap; to make up for the loss of income, they charge these agent a higher fee. It may not seem fair, but remember, the brokerage is there to MAKE MONEY, not friends. Many of these old-school brokerages don't want you to be at a certain production level because you'll become competition for the broker. You get to the point where you're paying so much in fees, it's more beneficial to buy your own brokerage. They don't want you doing that; they don't want you to go off on your own and become the competition. So, they have to try and keep you at a level that ensures you still need them but are productive enough to still make them money.

Let me tell you about an experience I had a few years ago. I had a team of agents, and we were ready to move onto a new office; the team I had built was growing fast, and I had started to become a problem for my current brokerage. I wasn't looking for anything in particular in a new office, just someone who wanted me to join them. So, I was at the interview, and I straight up asked the interviewer, "I just want a yes or a no. Where are we standing? Do you want me to join this office or not?"

The interviewer responded, "I'm going to tell you no, and this is why I don't want you in my brokerage. The first reason is that you live too far away, so you're not going to add any value to our office. You're not going to teach anything. You're not going to have an office here, and you're not going to have a presence. So, you're not adding any value by just being a part of our office." This office was looking for people who could contribute to their office, which I get, and I LOVE. I love it because if you can contribute, there's a mutually beneficial relationship between you and the brokerage.

He continued, "You'd be a burden on my system because if you're doing as many deals as you've done, and you continue to do that, it's not a profitable venture for us. You will put a stress on our system and on our administrative staff with the number of deals you're doing." That also made sense to me. They have to make money. He said that he was looking for people who just barely cap. Just barely pay their full fees. The broker needs cash flow each month. If an agent pays off their cap in a month, there won't be any cash flow out of that agent for the rest of the year. Many of these brokerages run month to month, so if there's no cash flow, there's no business.

Finally, he said, "The third reason I don't want you to join my brokerage is you're too ambitious. You're going to do something else." That's what I realized—the real estate brokerage models and the systems that I've been a part of were not designed for unlimited potential. Often, a brokerage will make it seem like that is what they are offering you, but in reality, there are limits to what they can provide. It's all "unlimited" within their system, but the system may be broken. So, make sure you do your research and really evaluate a brokerage to make sure it is right for you before you sign on the dotted line.

Really understand what you're bringing to the table and what the brokerage has to gain or lose from your success. Once you understand that, you can see how one brokerage over another may be better suited to you and your business. Examine this relationship and ask yourself if you are helping the brokerage more than the brokerage is helping you. If the brokerage asks you to go on a broker open house tour so they can say as an office, "We had this many people come through," it might be counterproductive to YOUR business plan. Taking the time to help the brokerage in ways that don't offer you any benefit will only take time away from the tasks that will actually bring in money for YOU. Remember, you are not an employee; you're an independent contractor. Make sure they aren't taking advantage of you and hindering your business.

Next, ask yourself, Are you getting all the services your brokerage offers? Are you taking advantage of the services? Make sure you know what is offered and take advantage of each and every benefit provided by the brokerage. You're paying for them, after all, so it only hurts you not to use them! I saved myself a lot of time and money when I started taking advantage of all the services that I had at my disposal.

Think about how much you are paying and what you're actually getting out of it. If you're in a situation where you end up paying so many fees and losing a percentage of your commission that you could use to start your own business with an office staffed with agents with the amount of money you're forking over to the brokerage, something needs to change. At the end of the day, you *can* always go off on your own (not that I would recommend it in most cases), so you need to evaluate what is important to you and if the brokerage you are with is aligned with that. Think about the benefits you gain from being with the brokerage and the fees or percentage of your commission you have to pay for those benefits. Is it worth it?

Ideally, a brokerage is there to protect and support you because you don't know what you're doing. To ensure that is the case, evaluate if you have unlimited potential for growth that is supported by the system is in place *and* if the brokerage actually wants it to happen. If you are working to plant the seeds of growth for your business, then you come to harvest and find out the brokerage does not support that size of a harvest, it causes problems for you and for them. So, picking the right broker is CRUCIAL to your long-term success.

The Purpose

What is your purpose? I'm sure that somewhere along the line, someone has asked you, "What is your purpose? Why do you do what you do, at a deeper level?" I think question translates almost directly into real estate. Seven out of 10 agents either quit or they're in what I call a *state of quit* within the first 12 months of getting in the business. The successful agents and brokers, I observe, have a clearly defined purpose in their lives.

We all deal with some drama in this business. For example, I take a lot of things personally that I shouldn't, but because I have a clear definition of what I'm doing in my life, I get through it. I'm not saying I enjoy it, but I get through it. It's important to be clear on your purpose and make sure your actions, each day, reflect and are aligned with your purpose and your life goals. Once you have that, everything else just falls into the minutia category; it just needs to be "taken care of." Don't dwell on the overwhelming thoughts, such as, "I can't even conceive of how I could do this appointment or this, or this, or this." Just get through it. It needs to happen, so focus your attention on that thought. If you don't know your purpose, get to know your purpose.

I once worked with a broker (we'll call him Paul, Paul with a Purpose) who really understood his purpose and how his real estate career would facilitate that. I really respected how Paul ran his business because it was very goal-oriented and aligned with his purpose. Not everybody can align their purpose with their real estate career. But Paul did.

At one point, Paul had a goal to open 10 offices, and each day, every activity and hour of he work put in fed into that goal. Once Paul met his goal, he not only impressed others in the real estate community with his dedication to the goal, but he was offered other opportunities to branch out into other realms, including training.

This opportunity (to become a trainer of sorts) included traveling to different countries and training agents around the world. Though this sounds like a wonderful opportunity, Paul's coach (it wasn't me at the time) reminded him that this opportunity did not align with his purpose. So, instead, he continued to focus on what would get him closer to his purpose, and he was successful in doing so.

That was very impressive. Paul knew that to go where he wanted to go with his business and his life, he had to approach his job in a certain manner. He was willing to do whatever it took to get there, and that's something I can appreciate. When distractions came up, it didn't take much for Paul to get back on course because he always had that greater purpose to focus on.

Time and time again, agents, brokers, and anyone involved in the real estate industry get distracted by "shiny objects" in and out of the business. It can be hard to get back on course and do the mundane day-to-day activities that will feed into your ultimate goals when there are more exciting, shiny things just sitting there, waiting to distract you.

Having a purpose brings out motivation on a whole different level; it awakens a whole different animal in a person because now, they're working toward something they believe in with their whole being. I love when I can see somebody's purpose in alignment with their real estate career because they are able to get through the mundane without being babysat, and they know what they need to do and actually do it. Of course, no man is an island, and you may need the occasional reminder to keep you on track, but that is what coaching and training groups are there for. You're able to stay on track when you surround yourself with people who stay on track as well. But we'll get into that more later on in the book. For now, just try and dig deep; think about what your purpose is and how your business aligns with it.

*   *   *

If you would like to schedule a complimentary consultation, please visit my website at www.brianernstcoaching.com.

Do You Have a Goal?

This is going to sound so simple it's ridiculous. Do you have a goal? Do you truly have a goal? Most people will respond with, "Yeah, I have a goal." Well, what is it? Are we talking about something that's specific, measurable, and actually attainable? Is it on a timetable? There are many different versions of smart goals out there, but does it fit the *basic criteria* of a goal?

What do you want? What do you want to accomplish with your great real estate success? Is it financial abundance? Is it the ability to do things with your family, spend time with friends? Do you have a clear, objective goal? Have you broken it down? What does it take to get to that point? Often, in real estate, it's the amount of money you make, a specific deal, or a combination of the two. So, ask yourself these questions and make sure you know what you're working toward. Don't just write down your dreams; write down the tangible goals that will get you to that dream you have.

Some examples of clear goals are:

- Make $100k in real estate sales,
- Close 36 deals a year,
- Gross or net profit of X number of dollars,
- X number of transactions

Make sure you are VERY clear on what the goal is and what it gets you. To this end, ask yourself if it is something that helps direct your actions. Do you look at it every day, multiple times a day, to keep it in the forefront of your mind? Do you have a vision board? I recommend you put one together if you don't. Having a visual representation of your goals placed in a prominent place in your workspace can help inspire you and keep your mind focused in the right direction.

It's simply amazing what happens when you put those images in your head every day. If your goals are unclear, what do you think your results are going to be? This is why it is important to take the time to write down and refine your goals. It sounds so simple, but it is critical to your success.

*   *   *

Want to discuss putting the 52 Secrets to work for you?
Schedule a complimentary consultation through my website at
www.brianernstcoaching.com. I would love to discuss your
options with you personally.

How to Open

Often, one of the roadblocks for agents is actually getting the conversation started with a potential client. So, I'm going to make it really easy for you and provide you with five questions to ask interested parties to initiate the conversation and keep them engaged so they become clients.

"So, when are you folks planning on moving?" This first question is an opener you can use with anybody, anywhere. You're not asking them, "Can I list your house? You want to sign up for a 30-year mortgage?" Just the simple question of when doesn't put any pressure on them other than friendly conversation. As a general rule, if they're moving in two years or less, they're in my hot file, meaning I'm going to stay in touch with them as much as I possibly can. When most people say two years, it's a year; when they say six months, it's three months. That's just been my experience. Obviously, you can decide for yourself how you want to handle each lead based on your business and experience.

The second question is, "How long have you owned your home?" This will continue to keep the person engaged while gathering information about their background to help you plan for their future if they do become a client. I'll often get a variety of answers to this because it's not just one question. It's multiple questions in one. They might not own their house; they might not even live in a house.

A great follow up if they say they don't own their house is to ask, "When does your lease end?"

It's that easy. Again, just another simple, non-threatening question that provides you with the information you need.

"Where did you move from?" This third question gets a little more in-depth with people, and it's a great way to engage them. If they're local, you can then try to connect and see if you have anything in common to build that deeper relationship.

The fourth question is, "If you could move anywhere, where would it be?" This really gets people thinking. Sometimes, they think big, responding with their eventual dream of retiring to Hawaii to live out the rest of their days with a mai tai in hand. Sometimes, they're thinking more immediate or practical, responding with answers that list good school districts and safe neighborhoods. Whichever way they go, it gives them an opportunity to share a bit more about themselves and give you more venues for engaging them further in the conversation or providing you with some talking points to bring up, say, in a year when you reach out to see if they have need of a real estate agent.

The last question is a follow-up to the fourth question and mirrors your opening question: "And when would that be?" We've now brought it back around to getting actionable answers from the person. The answer they give will provide you with a clear direction in how you continue your relationship with them, whether it's, "Wonderful, if you want, I can give you a call next week to go over your options," or, "That sounds great. Here's my card; feel free to give me a call when you're ready to start looking." And just like that, you've either got a client in the works or a lead for the future.

These questions are easy to ask, non-threatening, and you can ask them of anyone, anywhere without having to worry about it being appropriate in the setting or making the potential client uncomfortable. You can go through these questions anywhere—networking events, friendly gatherings, etc. They're harmless questions, but they are very useful for information gathering and relationship building.

Knowing Your Numbers

Do you really know your numbers? Meaning, do you know how many conversations you've had in the past day, week, month, year? Breaking that down, do you know how many *conversions* you had from those conversations; how many turned into listing and buyers' appointments? Do you know the lead sources from each of those appointments? Do you know how many properties you put under contract, how many deals fell apart? Do you know your conversion rate on every aspect of the real estate transaction?

These are all important questions you need to make sure you know the answers to. If you gather this information each week, you will have the numbers to help you make informed business decisions as you compare your results against each other. You can see what worked and what didn't work, and it will help you determine if you are on track for your annual and long-term goals.

One aspect of knowing your numbers is keeping track of the money you put into marketing and other business expenses. You need to have profit and loss statements for each year so you will know where your money is going and coming from and can make any adjustments necessary for the next year.

I worked with an agent who was one of the top agents in her area for sales and real estate. We'll say her name is Cindy (Cindy the Certified Agent). Cindy never really tracked her numbers. She was excellent at talking to people and converting and closing deals; she was all over social media and attended all the important events, really getting her name out there. But she didn't have an accurate portrait of where she was spending her money and how much she was actually making.

When I dug into her finances, I saw a much different story than the one social media would have you believe. She wasn't making nearly the amount of money she should be because she was spending most of the money she made on each deal. She paid for unnecessary business tools that she never used and over-paid those working for and with her. Her assistant was driving the same nice luxury vehicle she was, so you know something wasn't right!

Her inability to show with paper and numbers what she was actually taking in didn't only hurt her business because she wasn't managing her finances effectively, but it was hurting her personally as well. Her ex-husband was always trying to get more money for child support, because based on her gross commissions, it looked like she was raking in much more than she was. And don't even get me started on her taxes—they were a mess, and she was always behind on them. Cindy may have been good at making deals, but she was never going to have any long-term success if she couldn't get her finances straigented out to a point where she knew what she was spending money on and could plan for future success.

On one occasion, I opened up one of the W2s for the year that she hadn't yet opened because she thought it has been a rough year for her. Turns out she had made over $300,000 that year! Because she hadn't been tracking everything, it might have felt like a rough year because she didn't actually have all of those earnings in her bank account. Cindy had spent it all without realizing it, throwing money to needless expenses and not keeping track of the tax-deductible expenses that were actually necessary for her business.

Don't be like Cindy. Understand which expenses you make lead to deals and which expenses end up being fruitless. For example, if you spend money attending social events that only lead to one lead a year, cut back on those and focus your money where you know you can get more leads. At the end of the day, you want your business to be successful, and to do that, it has to make money. So, track all the ins and outs of your business and use that information to better your business and set it up for long-term success.

Consider your gross profit. What is your net? What are your costs? What is the breakdown of your expenses? What's tax deductible? What's not? And as an agent, there is a large percentage of daily costs that can be deducted as long as they are for the business (just make sure you follow the guidelines and are prepared for any audits).

When something isn't working in your business, it will be reflected in your profit and loss statements. But unfortunately, a profit loss statement is after the fact. You have to have an understanding of the numbers on a daily basis so you know what's coming. You need to know your numbers at each level. Know where your lead generation sources are and what they cost you. Remember to also factor in the cost of time. If you know your worth, you'll have this understanding and be able to easily factor in time to your weekly, monthly, and yearly reports.

I know one agent in particular in Texas who runs a large team, but he doesn't do a lot of marketing. He does most of his of lead generation through cold calling and other networking events with his team. So, he's had people on payroll, and when the numbers go down for a month, that payroll is still there, a steady expense to his business. If you don't know your numbers, you cannot cut out certain expenses or make adjustments ahead of time because you won't be able to forecast for those dips in the business. All the money in a real estate agent's bank account is the result of everything they've done in the past six months. Real estate deals don't happen overnight. If I list a house today, I'm not going to get paid today; even if the house sold the minute I listed it, that money won't be mine until all the paperwork is done. And it may have taken me months and months to nurture that relationship to even get to the point of listing the property.

I recommend everyone have a clear profit and loss statement every single month, so you know where you stand and can make sure you're on track for your yearly goals. Then, because each deal takes a different amount of time, I encourage agents to look at the past six months of their business so they have a better general idea of how the business is going overall and what the trends are in their successes and failures. If you feel like you're off track, you can just look at the data and adjust, if needed, or sleep better knowing you're doing what's right for your business. Don't be afraid to look at the data; it is there to serve you. So, look at it all. Once you have that information, you can better understand if something you did five months ago was worth it and decide whether or not to do it again. With the right information, you can plan better for the future and make smart, informed business decisions that will, ultimately, lead to success and the accomplishment of your goals. And that all starts with knowing your numbers.

Power Open House

I'm guessing if you're a human being and have been on this planet for a number of years, you're familiar with the real estate term open house. But are you familiar with what a POWER open house is? Probably not. A power open house is my version of what a lucrative open house can look like. It is basically an open house on steroids. A power open house not only provides the benefits of a traditional open house, but it also attracts business in other ways. My roots in real estate started with the power open house, and I've fine-tuned it over the years into the basic steps I'll provide to you so you can have your own successful power open house (or POH). When it's done right, a POH should increase the number of people attending your open house by a significant factor. We're talking 200%, 300%, or 400% more people coming through!

Advertisements and the marketing are an important part of a successful POH. The first and most crucial part of the power open house is making sure you get the signs right. I use a for sale sign that has my picture and my contact information on it.

Now, why do I do that? Think about it: If you were going to sell your home and you looked around at the other signs in the neighborhood and noticed one agent with 20 listings and 20 signs up, and you have another agent with one sign up, which agent would you be more likely to call? The sign is your opportunity to put your face and contact information in front of a whole neighborhood, area, or subdivision every single week, whether you have a listing in there or not, whether you're borrowing somebody's listing to do an open house or they are on your listing.

Now, you've got your name and your face on the sign; next, make sure that it is a for sale sign. Then, put the open house rider on it, a directional rider and with an arrow. I usually use another rider attached to it that lists the time and date of the open house. Make sure the clients and buyers you're trying to attract have all the information they need in one convenient place.

Quantity and placement are the next details that can make all the difference. For a power open house, I recommend a MINIMUM of 15 signs. Don't just set out all 15 signs on one corner; spread them around the neighborhood. Major intersections should have two to four signs so that people can see them in both directions. Then, add a few more along the way so people don't get lost and end up at another open house or decide to go somewhere else instead. Ideally, try to get permission to put the signs on the corner of the yards you want to target for visibility as far ahead of time as you can. If you don't get the homeowner's permission, you need to have time to prepare an alternative plan and location for your signs.

The next step is making sure that you have advertised this open house on the MLS and every major real estate website out there that you can advertise on to make sure it is exposed to anybody looking for open houses. It is important to get the word out to as many people as possible.

The next part of the power open house is making sure that you let the neighborhood know you're having an open house. Not only do you put a sign in the yard where the open house is at, but you go should go door-to-door as well. Knocking on the neighbors' doors is one of the easiest things to do because you're not actually selling them anything. If you do it for an hour in the evening during the weekdays, imagine how many homes and homeowners you can get in front of. The script for this task is simple and easy. You knock on their door, and invite them to the open house! Say, "I know some people may be uncomfortable looking at their neighbors' homes because they're not really going to buy it, but I want to invite you to come and take a look. If you have friends and family who want to look too, please come on by." When they DO come to the open house, they're more likely to engage in a conversation because they've already met you and seen your sign with your face on it all over the place.

You want to make sure you control the situation for everyone who comes through the open house. This means when they come in, they sign in and you get all their contact information before they get any information about the house or even have a chance to look at it. One of the easiest ways that I've done this is by saying, "Look, the sellers asked me to make sure that we have a record of everybody who comes in, so please sign in. You know, I'm just doing this at the seller's request." Visitors will usually understand a seller wanting to know who is looking at their house, so they won't feel like you're pressuring them to give you their information so you can bother them later. And if they're with an agent, that's a whole other story! Just let the potential buyer tour the house with their agent and be available to answer any questions they may have.

Once you have their information, give them a flyer about the property and let them go through the property. It's pretty stress-free. Then ask them the five questions from Secret 9!

So, to fully leverage an open house, follow these steps to make it a power open house and build your future client base in the process.

Don't Handle Buyers

The last statistic I heard from the National Association of Realtors stated that the average amount of time realtors spend with a buyer is 24 and a half hours, and the average time they spend with a seller is only eight hours. Now, I know that statistic has changed over the years, but the amount of hours spent with buyers versus sellers has always been significantly higher. When you think about it more, you realize how many listings you could have worked on in the same amount of time spent handling buyers. So, to increase your productivity and success, DON'T HANDLE BUYERS! This will save you SO much time throughout your career.

When you go on a listing appointment, how often is it actually necessary that you physically go to the property? The buyer's side of any listing has more going on with it, which, by the nature of the work, means more time spent. When I first got into real estate, one of the first things I realized is the amount of hours that go into helping a buyer versus a seller. Then, regardless of the amount of time you spend with them, it won't matter much if there isn't a contract in place and they decide to go with someone else.

I was actually fairly efficient with getting buyers into houses in a timely manner when I first started out. No matter how efficient I was, it still took WAY more time listing a house, and I knew my time was not being spent in the best way for my business. I was handling both buyers and sellers, and it got to a point where I knew I couldn't continue as I had been.

I had helped this one particular buyer and was under contract with three different properties when, for three completely unrelated reasons, they all fell apart. One was ridiculous home inspection stuff. With the second, the seller was still in a lawsuit with the previous buyer, which they had kicked out of the deal. The judge ordered them to put the deal back together even though we were in a contract and all squared away on the legal front, but the judge didn't clearly understand that. The fight would have taken too long and wasn't worth it. The third deal, honestly, fell apart in a way that was so unremarkable, I don't even remember how it happened, but it was the final straw for that buyer. All the reasons were different, unrelated reasons, and I don't blame the buyer for it, but it still happened. And after all of it, the buyer decided to buy a for sale by owner without me. That was *my* final straw; that's when I decided I was done with buyers. Not only did the whole ordeal hurt personally but also financially because I wasted my time with nothing to show for it. So, I knew I didn't want to work with buyers, and I changed my business model.

There are a few different ways you can save yourself the time of working with buyers without it hurting your business. The first is having a referral source. You can do it anytime, anywhere, and still get paid on the referral, but you've saved even more time. A referral fee to another agent is often around 25%. When you look at the long-term effects of the time spent with the buyers, you realize it is actually is more advantageous to just focus on sellers, refer out the buyer, collect 25%, and not run around with the buyers all the time. You make much LESS money running around showing properties than you do simply referring the buyer to someone else and collecting your 25%. Don't forget to continue to nurture that relationship for future deals so they return to you as a client. The agent is helping you, but that buyer is still a potential moneymaker for you; you just don't have to spend the time showing them properties to cash in.

The second way to avoid working with buyers is what I've done for most of my career, and that is to use a buyer's agent. I let my buyer's agents handle all my buyers, buyer leads, and anything else that has to do with buyers. I don't show houses at all. It has saved me so much time and provided a way to better control how I spend my time. Sure, you split the profits with the buyer's agent, but the lost income is far less significant than the time lost doing all the work yourself.

Some people ask me, "Brian, why didn't you get buyers who were spending more money?" Because the amount of amount of time involved was too great. As I was restructuring my business the second time, I was working a crazy amount of hours handling buyers. That year, I made about $400,000 in gross commissions handling buyers and sellers, but I was killing myself doing that. It was good money, but I literally didn't have time to eat. I mean, I lost so much weight because I was just working. I worked. I worked some more, worked some more, went to bed, and got up and did it all over again. There was no eating in that schedule.

So, I realized early on that I couldn't keep that up, and I got a buyer's agent. I went through a few buyer's agents until I got my first one that really worked out and impacted my business. Right before I hired her, I was making around $300,000. After that first full year with her, I made $200,000 because I paid her about $100,000. So, I went from $300 to $200 bringing her on. But since I could focus more on the listing side of it, that next year, I was at $400,000. I may have lost some money that first year, but it was an investment in future success. I was able to spend the year developing my marketing tools and listings and nurturing relationships. I ended up with way more listings that following year and basically doubled my business from the year before. My investment paid off.

Lastly, instead of a buyer's agent, some people will use a showing assistant whose job it is to just handle showing properties instead of the entire transaction. For some people, that is the better solution because they still want to be involved with the buyers but want to save the time that showing properties takes.

Not handling the buyers gave me the freedom and flexibility I didn't have before, and it can do the same for you. You'll no longer have to run out and show a house last minute because there'd been a multiple offer situation and time was of the essence. It is always a rush and a panic, and I don't want to live my life in such a frantic state. I'd rather be on the other end of it, saying, "Yeah, we'll get to you in the morning, we'll get back to you." There is no hurry.

It may be exciting at first, but the excitement always dies down. Sometimes, the buyer will be so anxious to get going that everything has to be done NOW, and then, they decide they don't want the place anymore, or their loan falls through, or whatever scenario you can imagine. Then, all that adrenaline coursing through your body comes to a stop, and you're left emotionally and physically drained. All that work and hype for nothing. You've got no money to show for your work, and you've put yourself into a place of exhaustion where putting in more work with the next buyer seems untenable.

If I had to do my career over again from the start, I'd make it so I'd never work with a buyer. But I'd still have a system in place to help buyers because I am running a real estate business, after all. I want the message I portray to be one of help: "Come to me with all your real estate needs. I will help you out with that." But just because I offer to help doesn't mean I have to do the work myself. I can still provide the best care for people by providing them with the resources or avenues to accomplish their real estate goals.

It's like going to the doctor. When you go to the doctor, does the doctor just give you a shot, or does the nurse give you the shot? You don't have to do it all; you just have to be the one who knows what's going on. You can still provide care without having to hold the needle. Not handling buyers can save you more time and increase your business. If you've picked the right clients, you can basically work real estate as a part-time job because you never have to be 100% available—there's nothing that urgent on that side of the equation.

Remember, there are different solutions and different systems that work for each real estate agent, so I'm not saying you *have* to get a buyer's agent like I have. What I am saying, however, is that you should do whatever works best for you and ensure you don't have to handle buyers.

*　　*　　*

Want to discuss putting the 52 Secrets to work for you?
Schedule a complimentary consultation through my website at
www.brianernstcoaching.com. I would love to discuss your
options with you personally.

Mailing Advertisements

At the beginning of my career, I was broke, and I certainly didn't have any money to spend on advertisements of any sort. I believe the first year I was in real estate, I made 40 grand in commissions, and my expenses were just over 40 grand, so do the math. How much money did I make in my first year in real estate? It wasn't particularly impressive. The next year, it was better, as I started to get better with open houses and direct advertisements. In this day and age, mailing advertisements might seem like a thing of the past, but they can really help improve your business if done right.

When I got into the business almost 16 years ago, direct advertisements were the most effective way to get in the door and find a listing. It was a little cheaper back then, and then it went away much faster than I thought it would after the market crashed. Now, the majority of people are finding homes on the internet and are finding leads in one way, shape, or form through the internet. I still find, however, that many sellers want to know who their local expert is, who really knows their area, and the direct mailings can help you with that visibility.

I started doing direct mailing advertisements at the beginning of my career, and I still do them today. But I do it in a smart way that complements the new climate we live in. One thing to focus on as you do these mailings is making sure the cost of the direct advertisements don't outweigh the money you make from them. For every dollar you spend on direct mailing marketing, you should be making $10 in return. It doesn't always work out the first year or so, so you have to be patient. And it's not something that you can just do on a whim here and there and expect results. It's something that needs to be consistent, with a plan in place that results in sending something out, at a minimum, 12 times a year and once a month. If you're really looking to break into a neighborhood, it's going to take more than that because you want to be at the forefront of these homeowners' minds. So, make sure you know what your goal is for the advertising campaign and are realistic about the current visibility you have in a given neighborhood.

These direct mailing advertisements have contributed to the majority of my income in real estate because most of my income has come from the listing side of things. There are times where a mailing campaign does not work as well, and you might need to adjust. That is par for the course. Just focus on the area you want to market to, and make sure you know what the benefits of marketing in that area are.

Do those people see your marketing in multiple ways? Do they see the advertisements on your car? The mailing campaigns are only one part of the equation, and you need to make sure you are reaching your potential clients in at least three different ways. Either you've physically knocked on their door, they've seen your open house signs or car with advertisements, or they've received direct mailing advertisements. You can't just randomly send mail to a few neighborhoods here and there. You have to examine the area and make sure it fits into the right criteria that will better ensure your success.

Once you've identified the right area to advertise to, you need to plan out what the mailing will say and how it will look. You want to let the neighborhood know YOU are their neighborhood specialist. Plan out your message, then decide if it will be a postcard, a letter, etc. and what kind of paper will be used. Those small details can make a huge difference.

The majority of what I use are high-gloss postcard mailings. They're bigger than the average souvenir postcard and very colorful. I make sure to include a very clear call to action and information on how to reach out. "Call today for your free market analysis." What do they do? People pick up the phone and call. I don't really want them to go to a website. I don't want them to text me; I want them to call. Over the phone, I'm able to start building the rapport that is hard to build via text. While on the phone, I'm able to properly qualify them for that appointment and build the relationship necessary for future business.

In a world where people are faced with different images and information thrown at them through every screen, it can offer you a way to stand out and simplify things for them. With an engaging message, a simple postcard can transform your business as part of a larger direct mailing advertisement campaign.

Refrigerator Magnets

The title of this secret is refrigerator magnets. Now, if I've lost you at this point, stick with me a bit longer because this is all going to make sense. Now, why are refrigerator magnets a part of a 20-hour work week? If you put important information on that magnet, whatever it may be, most people feel like they need to have it, whatever it is. They stick it on their refrigerators, the front, the side, and most importantly, they keep it. They now have my face on the their fridge, and it's there for however long they keep it. THAT'S the point that I want to make.

If you have an item that you can send to somebody and they keep it, it's AMAZING how that can come up in the future. I've had people say, "I know I've seen your face somewhere, I just can't figure out where I know you from." One time, this guy saw my face from his girlfriend's house in a neighborhood where I advertise. He went to one of my open houses, and he swore he knew me. Though I didn't send any mailings to his neighborhood, we were able to figure out that his girlfriend lived in one of my target areas. So, these magnets end up having a farther reach than just my target area because they're in a visible, prominent part of the house that occupants and guests alike will visit.

In the past, I've clearly seen my refrigerator magnets on listing appointments that were from two to 15 years ago! Were these magnets directly correlated to me getting the listing appointment? Maybe not directly, but it was certainly influential because any other advertisements I sent only reinforced the fact that they are looking at me on their refrigerator every day, whether that affects them consciously or subconsciously.

It's incredible what *items of value* I can give to somebody that they're going to keep and place somewhere they will see often. Refrigerator magnets have been the best for me for that type of purpose.

I have to admit, when I go to a listing appointment, the first place my eyes travel to, once in the kitchen, is the refrigerator. I can spot my refrigerator magnets a mile away because I know what I'm looking for. It's kind of like when you buy a new car and you suddenly see that car all over the place. I see my magnets all the time, and it works for my clients too. They see my face on their fridge when they get a glass of water, then they see it again as they drive by my house with my branded car parked out front on their way to work.

People will keep magnets for a long time because they don't take up any space and can even be used to hold up a pride-inducing report card or the all-important to-do list. When I have to cut back on certain advertisements, either because of the market or the results of it, I know magnets are the one thing people will keep, so I don't skimp here. Yes, they cost a little bit more, but they're worth it. Number one, the targets keep it. Number two, if they don't keep it, they will often feel bad about throwing it out. I'll take the guilt route! If they feel guilty about that and remember my name and my face with that, I'll take it! I've actually had people say, "I feel bad about throwing your magnets out," while I'm sitting at their kitchen table listing their house. They remembered me!

Now, if you can think of a better item you can mail to somebody directly in the same price range that they either keep or feel bad about throwing out, let me know. In the meantime, think about making the small investment in yourself and purchasing some refrigerator magnets; their reach will blow you away.

Social Media

Social media can be a big asset to your business, but it can also be a problem if you don't set up some guidelines. So, I've got a few guidelines that I follow and that I suggest for you to make your social media work *for* you.

The first rule is to block out specific time for working on your social media accounts. I've found that I can easily be sucked in and lose time on social media. So, I set up time specifically for social media, then once that time is up, I don't touch it again until the next scheduled time. Remember how important and valuable your time is; you have other things you need to do in your day, and you shouldn't spend all your time on one avenue of your business.

The next rule is to be selective about who you follow and whose posts you comment on. If the person that posts is a potential lead, comment then follow them and respond to them. Only target people who are going to bring in new business or who are a part of your our current business. That's who I follow and who I try to connect with. By focusing strictly on people who are potential lead sources or referral sources for you, you essentially train Facebook to highlight those peoples' posts for you and not fill up your news stream with people who are not leads for you.

If you need help identifying who those people are, look to your client and lead database. Those are the people you should reach out to and follow. Everyone else falls to the side. Then, once you've got that list together, look at the kinds of things they post and use your instincts based on what you know about each person. You should be focused on getting referrals from these people or potentially converting them into future clients, so you want to make sure you're not focusing on the wrong people.

The third rule is to keep your messages short and engaging. You want to catch their eye with a graphic or well-used colors. You don't want the actual text to be too long or verbose because they will keep on scrolling. Short, simple, and engaging—that's the recipe for success. My posts have the sole purpose of trying to connect with the people I think can help my business. Once you've gotten them engaged, try to move the conversation to the phone where you can really start to build that relationship.

Finally, take advantage of paid promotional advertisements through Facebook, LinkedIn, and any of the social media platforms. Examine the engagement stats each platform provides to make sure your advertising hits your database and your target market, and you're effectively relaying the message you want. Take advantage of the hyper-targeting available within Facebook where you can target by specific demographic and psychographics as well as geographical factors. You want your social media advertising to mirror your physical advertising so you have multiple avenues to reach your potential clients.

Remember, limit your time, focus your targeting, keep it simple, and take advantage of the advertising tools available on each social media platform. If you follow these rules, you can make social media work for you and make a big difference in your marketing campaigns.

Outside Influence

I used to get criticisms and critiques from other agents as I grew my business. It bothered me, and it distracted me. I thought that I wasn't doing something the right way. In reality, I was just growing parts of my business and probably taking parts of their business away. The point I'm trying to make is that it won't do you any good to focus on the criticism, and you have to learn to ignore it if you want to keep your sanity. Ignore any criticism from those people who are not directly involved with your business, and have your own best interest in mind for growth and profit.

I spent years doing this. You want to have a good, healthy relationship with the agents you work with and deal with day to day. Don't get tied up in the drama that they might try to pull you into. If it's constructive feedback that you can use to grow your business, that's one thing; listen and put the information to use as you see fit. But if they're *just* criticizing you, don't bother. Ask yourself if what they're saying is going to make you more money. Is it going to put you in front of more sellers to get listings? Is it going to put you in front of more leads?

If it's not, ignore it. There are so many subjects within real estate that you could get caught up in and so many different personality types that have various opinions and ideas. Focus on what's best for building your business. You don't have to do everything people suggest, and you don't have to be everything to everyone.

One agent I've worked with over the years has a particular pattern. As soon as we get in a deal, she starts asking for the world for her client. We would have a property under contract and an agreed-upon deal, but she would still continue to ask for things for her client. She would get on me, make personal attacks, and do whatever she could to provoke a response from me. I finally started ignoring her whenever this situation would arise. If it didn't have to do with license law or any obligation, legal or otherwise, that I had to handle, I just started ignoring it.

Once I did that, she stopped asking, and my deals went a lot smoother and much quicker. I spent less time with that particular agent, and I had time to better prepare my client for dealing with her.

People will always try to make your business their business, so you have to make a concerted effort to ignore and block out the negative and focus solely on what will actually help you and your business thrive. In the end, you'll save yourself time and frustration, and your business can only benefit from that.

Average Person

Jim Rohn stated, "You're the average of the five people you spend the most time with." In regard to real estate, who are those five people if you had to identify them? Are they bringing you up, challenging you? Are they working at a higher level than you are? Are they positive? Uplifting? Finding new and better ways to do things? Are they having fun with what they do? Are they profitable? Are they working less than 20 hours a week?

Most of the time, agents hang out with people who aren't doing deals because they've got time on their hands. But that's only going to influence you in a way that could bring your productivity down. The people who are doing deals on a regular basis are the ones you should be hanging out with. If you're not hanging out with them right now, you might want to consider finding some new people.

I know that may sound harsh, but it was one of the fundamental adjustments that, once I implemented, changed my real estate career. I changed the people who I spent time with and the people I worked with to improve my career. I still do that today. If someone is bringing me down or affecting my business negatively, I remove them from my inner circle. It's not worth it to waste time and energy on people who only drag you down.

I want to work with people who are better than me in real estate, who can do it better, who may know a better way. Then, I'm inspired to be better myself. If I hung out with a bunch of people who only did six deals a year, what would that do for me?

I challenge you to look at the people who you spend the most time with.

Let me tell you a story from Jack Canfield, author of *The Success Principles*. Jack's partner, Mark Victor Hansen, was making a good deal of money at the time. He was making in the millions a year. He had a good business going with Jack, selling books, booking speaking engagements, and arranging other endeavors. One day, Mark was on a TV networking circuit type of thing, and he was in a group with Tony Robbins. Mark approached Tony and said, "Tony, we do essentially the same thing. We do speaking events, we sell products, stuff like that. But the amount of money that you make is ridiculous compared to the amount of money I make."

And Tony responded, "Are going to a mastermind group?"

Mark assured Tony that he was.

"So, what's the average income of the people in your mastermind group?"

"Two, three, four million, something like that."

Tony continued, "That's my point. You're surrounding yourself with the SAME people. I'm in a mastermind group that requires you to have made at least $500 million annually. I don't qualify to get in the group because of my income. They allowed me to be in their group where the average person in that group was probably making a billion plus a year. And thus, I was surrounding myself with way more successful people where I could learn and observe how they were handling their businesses."

For Mark Victor Hansen, that idea was shocking. He wondered who those people were and how he could surround himself with them.

Ideally, you're around people who are making more money than you are, but it doesn't have to be about more money. It could be a quality that you want to have in yourself. It can be a skillset that somebody else has. And what do those qualities of the people you surround yourself with create for you, your lifestyle, and your happiness? It is not all about money. Money just provides opportunity and options.

If you had all the opportunities in the world, what would you really want to be doing? And who are those people you're going hanging out with? If you are able to surround yourself with people who have qualities or success markers that you aspire to, you will start picking up on some of those qualities that got those people to their points of success. So, make sure that when you average out the people you spend the most time with in real estate, they are those who can help elevate you instead of keeping you at the level you're currently at or even bringing you down.

But how can you do this? How do you find the people who can bring you up? One way is through mastermind groups. Another one is going to large events where you can network and meet people. When I go, I don't have to do much but talk to other people. I know the quality of the people in the room, and I know if they have the cash for the VIP tickets, they're on the level I want to engage with. All those people are motivated to make money, and they want to share that. So, invest in the VIP tickets and gain access to those people who can help you. Don't just go to go. Don't be a tourist. Really involve yourself and get the most out of these events.

I'm not the most comfortable in social situations. It's just not me. But if I just literally have to show up, I've won half the battle. Half of life is just showing up. The other half is what you do once you're there. So, for myself, my motivation is just do half of it—just do the showing up part because the other part will come. Sometimes, it doesn't, and that's okay because it gives you the experience to make it that much easier to do the next time. Often, just showing up to certain situations has allowed me to be in a place where somebody approaches me or I get into a conversation I never thought I'd get into, which eventually leads to something totally different. Each of these experiences has helped me grow.

Another way to find new people is just to simply put yourself out there—put your hopes and desires out into the world, and you'll attract a lot of those people to your world. Recently, I did something as simple as wishing someone a happy Mother's Day. This woman is someone who runs a coaching business, and we've connected in the past. On this occasion, she gave me some great ideas that came organically out of the casual connection we were having. It wasn't a formal coaching session or anything, just two people talking. Yet, I gain valuable insight and continued to grow that relationship to the betterment of me and my business.

I'm still happy I'm connected with that coach because a short conversation led to some brilliant ideas. I wouldn't have gotten those ideas from someone who was at the same place as me because, at that point, it's just like talking to a wall. You're not going to get any new feedback, and you might as well be talking to yourself. I like to be challenged on things, and I like to challenge myself. And if you surround yourself with the right people, they encourage it, they help it, and they help you get to the next level just through their advice, their information, or their connections. If you have those five people who you can turn to and seek guidance from, you'll be set. Make sure to nurture those relationships, and you'll be better off for it.

* * *

Want to discuss putting the 52 Secrets to work for you? Schedule a complimentary consultation through my website at www.brianernstcoaching.com. I would love to discuss your options with you personally.

Paperless

If you don't have a paperless office, stop reading this book RIGHT NOW and get your office set up right away. Going paperless will save you so much time! Enable online signatures for everything, whether with Dotloop, DocuSign, or any other similar program.

These days, everything is online, so at your listing appointment, use your tablet or computer to have your clients sign the contract right then and there. You can email them a copy, and everyone will be good to go. It works the same with buyers, so be prepared to go that route.

If you're not utilizing online signatures, how much time are you wasting? Just the fact that you have to run all over town to get paperwork signed should be reason enough why you should be using virtual contracts. The first deal I ever did took all day just to get all the paperwork filled out and signed properly, including multiple trips to and from the office to turn paperwork in. If I had just been able to have my client email his or her online signatures, I would have saved so much time and gas money!

Go paperless with your market analyses as well. Instead of printing off 100 pages of information your clients will never look at, provide it in an online format where you can go over the highlights with them on your tablet. Then, you can send it to them, and they will have it saved on their computers, available for viewing at any time and not getting lost amongst all their other paperwork. In the past, I've had clients ask me about a market analysis and about the price of something, and I responded, "I don't remember what I printed for you. I don't remember what I said because it's been so long." With a paperless system, you have a record of what you've shared with them and when, which can really help when those questions come up.

There is an agent I know who does so many deals that she has a driver drive her to her different appointments all day long. While she is in the car, she works on the market analysis on her tablets and is then ready when she gets to the next location to show it to her clients. When she gets there, she presents it on her tablet, sends the client a copy of it, and when they're ready to sign, she is able to pull up that screen and get their signature right on her tablet. It's so convenient.

If you operate paperlessly, you have all your information in one spot. Access to all of your documents is available at the touch of a finger or stylus. If it's in the cloud and you lose your phone, computer, or tablet, you still have access to it. And trust me, not spending hours searching for documents in your office will save you so much time.

Going paperless isn't just about turning all your contracts into online documents, but it can also help limit the items you think need to be printed so you don't invest time and energy into something that isn't worth it, like a brochure for buyers. One of my coaching clients, Audrey (Audrey the Agent), got a listing, and then, in my opinion, she wasted time focusing on all the wrong pieces.

Audrey then decided she wanted to make brochures. Now, brochures don't sell houses. Houses sell houses. If anything, brochures are just something that the seller can complain about, saying that it isn't pretty enough or doesn't meet their expectations. My job as an agent is to get people in the door. I am the listing agent; while buyers are working with the buyer's agent, and I usually do not have any direct communication with that buyer in any way, shape, or form because I represent the seller. So, I focus on getting them in the door. That's the job.

To encourage Audrey to ditch the brochures and focus her time and energy (and money!) elsewhere, I told her, "We, as a company, have decided to go green. Prospective buyers can look at your brochure online 24 hours a day, seven days a week. All they have to do is type in your address because it's everywhere, because of how the marketing works. The brochure is right there."

I further expanded and said, "It's just another piece of paper. Look, you're killing young baby trees to produce this paper. KILLING BABY TREES!"

I find this hilarious because sometimes people really want to put a brochure out there, but honestly, it's just a waste. Potential buyers already have the brochure walking in because they have all the information as well as a virtual brochure available to them online, on their phones.

Look for ways to cut back on your paper usage, and you'll find that most of the items you print and pass out currently aren't worth the ink they're printed with. Move all your contracts and any other paperwork that you can into a paperless system. You'll save time, money, and hassle in the end.

Clean Office

How organized is your office? Can you see your desk? Is it so bad that you've now moved into another room or office because your office has taken over as a whole new entity? I know some people who have done that. I meet with them and say, "Your office is a mess." They casually respond, "Oh, this isn't even my office. My office is next door." Or sometimes, it's, "Oh, you can't even get in the door in that one."

Yikes.

When you're not organized, when your desk is full of clutter, are you really ready for that new business to come in? Same goes for your car. I've seen people put stuff in their car, in their office, wherever, because they're just not ready for new business. It's a subconscious thing. If their spaces appear full, subconsciously, they think they're too busy or overloaded for new business. Once you clear out the clutter, clear out your car, clear off your desk, clear out your office, it's amazing how business starts to come in differently. With a fresher mindset and a clean business space to reflect that, you're ready for new business. You are no longer avoiding or procrastinating the work that has to be done to grow your business.

Sometimes, when my desk gets out of control, I take a box, hold it next to my desk, then take my arm and shove everything on my desk into that box. I just clear the whole desk off. I put the box under my desk, and I get back to work. After weeks of never looking in the box again, I'm able to realize what items I don't actually need, even though it all seemed important at the time.

Brian Ernst

So, ready yourself for new business and ready your mentality. Don't let whatever part of your subconscious that is trying to keep you down win. Clean your desk, clean your office, clean your car, and ready yourself for success.

Secret 21

The Frog

In Brian Tracy's book, *Eat That Frog,* he talks about Mark Twain's advice, saying if you have to do something today, do the hardest thing first. Do your most difficult task first thing in the morning. Now, if you have a list of your top five things to do, which one do you do first? According to the book, eat the ugliest frog first. That piece of advice makes my day so much easier; when I can get that thing out of the way, whatever it may be, the rest of the day feels that much more manageable. When I get that first hard thing out of the way, I am more productive because I'm not wasting time trying to avoid the task. I'm no longer procrastinating. Instead, I go through my day feeling lighter and more accomplished. And I'm always so surprised at how much I get done.

But what usually happens to people when they save their most difficult task for the end of the day? For me, it just doesn't get done. Eat that frog, and if you have multiple frogs to eat, eat the ugliest one first. Get it done, and move on with your day.

Do you have that list of the top five tasks you want to accomplish each day? What are they? I suggest writing them down the night before so you know what you're going to do that next day. Subconsciously, you may be thinking about it overnight and how you're going to get it done because you're visualizing it the night before. It's amazing how quickly you can get that done when you've planned to do it the night before.

One of my coaching clients, Pam (Pam the Procrastinator), had been struggling in her career. So, amongst other advice, I told her to try and do her hardest tasks first in the day. Eat that frog; eat the biggest, ugliest frog first. For her, that frog was prospecting; it was the phone calls to get new business. So, I told her to do it first thing in the morning. Now, is that the best time to get ahold of people? No, it's statistically not. But by the time it *is* statistically a better time to call, most people, including Pam, don't have the motivation to actually make the calls. When she finally did start doing that, her business doubled. Her business doubled!

Now, I can't guarantee that your business will double, but I can promise you it will only improve your attitude toward working every day, which can have greater impacts throughout all aspects of your life. So, eat that big, ugly frog, and get on with your day!

Basic Training

Years ago, I was coaching a very experienced real estate agent. The business he had was very impressive. When I broke down his numbers with him, I realized something that never crossed my mind in the beginning. He didn't have any basic real estate sales training. He was very good at getting in front of people. He got the gist of the whole process, obviously; he'd done it enough times. But he didn't have the basic real estate sales training.

Do you have basic real estate sales training? Now, we're talking the BASICS. How to lead generate, how to go through a listing appointment, how to go through a buyer appointment from start to finish, etc. What I've found is when agents, even the veteren agents who are the best in the business, are struggling and their businesses are not going the way they want them to, a simple way to reset is to get BACK TO THE BASICS. You don't need to take any advanced or upper-level courses; make sure your basics are where they should be first. If you haven't done this yet, there are some great programs out there, and I would love to talk to you to recommend what would work best for you.

* * *

If you would like to schedule a complimentary consultation, please visit my website at www.brianernstcoaching.com.

Waiting to Sell

When is the best time to sell your home? There are a variety of answers for this. Many people say it's in the spring. Some people think it's the summer. Pick a time of the year! But, in reality, neither answer is right. If anybody ever asks you that question, the answer is a simple "NOW." I can't be any clearer than this. NOW is the best time to sell.

We can't go back in time and sell our homes or their homes when things were either better or different or more accommodating to their needs. I'm not aware of anyone who can fully predict the future, so that's out of the question as well. Things can go up, and things can go down. Interest rates go up, and interest rates go down. All we truly know is where we're at now.

I had some clients who, when they first thought about selling, were holding out to get $5,000 more for their place before they would be willing to sell. *Five grand more.* They wanted to make sure it was worth five grand more. Then, the market crashed, and the property value went the other direction. Now, this was a newlywed couple living in a 1,100-square-foot townhouse. About six years later, when they became my clients, they now had two children and their in-laws living with them in that 1,100-square-foot townhouse. It was nuts. They were busting at the seams all because they insisted on waiting. Their agent gave them some bad advice at the time. The agent recommended they wait and sell in the spring, and the couple paid the price.

So, when they became my clients, I got them all the money they wanted and more. And I was able get them the house that they wanted. That was what was the most important thing to them, and that's what

Brian Ernst

I was concerned about. An extra few grand isn't worth all the troubles that waiting can bring.

NOW is the best time to sell. If anybody ever asks you that question, NOW is the best time to sell your home.

The Four Dollar-
Productive Activities

I've asked myself, "Is what I'm doing right now actually going to help me get to where I want to go?" It's kind of a broad question. A better question is, "Is what I'm doing a dollar-productive activity?" Most people don't understand what those are. Now, for me, a dollar-productive activity is very simple.

Am I listing a home?
Am I selling a home?
Am I negotiating on a property?
Am I prospecting?

Those are the four dollar-productive activities. Listing, selling, negotiating, and prospecting. If I'm not listing a home, I'm not selling a home, and I'm not negotiating a home, what am I doing? When I ask myself that question, I'm able to look at a task or project that I'm doing and determine if it is really worth it. Maybe someone else can do this for me; maybe there's a service out there that can accomplish this task for me. Then, once I've passed those non-productive tasks off, I'm able to focus on the four dollar-productive tasks that are the bread and butter of my business.

Listing, selling, negotiating. If you're not doing any of those three things, then you're prospecting. Now, if you want to work a full-time job and work the standard 40 hours a week, you should be filling each of those 40 hours with a dollar-productive activity. So, if you're not listing, selling, or negotiating, then you're doing 40 hours of what? Prospecting, lead generation. If you did 40 hours of consistent hours lead generation a week, think about the possibilities of where your business can go. Ask yourself this: "Is what I'm doing a dollar-productive activity?" Ask that question daily and throughout the day.

I was at an event one night, and the people there knew me as a real estate agent and knew I run a real estate team, but they also knew me for being a real estate coach. One group of people I was talking to were all surprised to find out that the majority of things I do during the week, in regard to coaching, have nothing to do with actually coaching anybody. They have to do with something else. It's the same with my real estate business. The majority of my time is not spent on appointments. It's spent on prospecting and lead generation, and even that, I've learned to condense steps and manage time better with time-saving systems in place.

In the coaching business, the majority of the time, it's the same. The majority of my time is spent doing lead generation, marketing, and prospecting. At some point, you already have the basic skill set of being a real estate agent. After that point, you have to focus on dollar-productive activities. Remember Secret 22, Basic Training? Most people don't really have the basics in place, which means the four dollar-productive activities aren't their main focus. It's everything else.

I think of it like a doctor. Is a doctor studying to be a doctor every single day? No, they're out there practicing medicine. And yes, they do learn and study here and there. They go to conferences, attend talks by renowned specialists, etc. And that's how I approach my coaching. I go to trainings, coaching myself on a regular basis; I actually spend a fortune on doing that each year—the events, the training, the actual coaching that I receive, it all adds up. But all of that isn't the main focus of my time; it's stuff I do periodically to keep me at the top of my game but not what I focus on 40 hours a week.

Unfortunately, the majority of agents who I've coached have not been productive in the sense of doing dollar-productive activities. It really comes into the 80/20 rule, the Pareto Principle. Twenty percent of the activity produces 80% of the results. So, to be successful, the 20% of your time that produces 80% of your results should be 80% of your time spent to produce even more results. And if people would actually do that, they would triple, quadruple, quintuple their businesses in the same or less amount of time.

In other words, if you look at the time you spend and realize that 20% of it is what's really generating income, instead of the 80% spent doing busy work or less productive tasks, you might be able to make some adjustments. When agents can look at the 20% that's very productive and expand on it, they'll start to experience growth.

So, focus on those four dollar-productive activities, and you'll start to see the growth in your business.

Sold Signs

When you put a property under contract, do you do anything special with your signs that you (should!) have in front of the property? For years, I'm sure you've seen people put signs on their properties. Now, it's technically not sold until it closes. In some areas, some boards don't approve of sold signs anymore. You may need to use an under contract sign instead.

So, are you advertising to the neighborhood with one of the cheapest ways to do to get more listings? Because who do you think will want to work with you next? It's going to be the people next door or down the street, the ones who see that you just sold their neighbor's property.

I've received countless phone calls that start off with, "Hey, I just saw you sold my neighbor's property. We are also thinking about moving."

When I first started in the business, I was told that you don't want to put sold signs up because you lose buyers by doing that. But remember, I don't really want the buyers. I want sellers. The best way to get sellers is to show them that you're actually selling properties. It's a simple step, but make sure to put that sign up as quickly as you can. You never know how many neighbors may be ready to sell their home, and by putting up the sold sign, they now know you can do it for them.

Think about it. If you're looking to sell your home, what number are you going to call? The one on the sign that's been sitting there unsold for six months, or the one that's got the sold sign on it? Results matter, so if you can put a sign up to advertise yours, you'll easily catch the eye of a potential client.

If you're in an area where you can't put a sold sign up, put an under contract or contract pending sign up; just put something up. It's really simple. Put a sign up!

Branding Your Sign

Let's talk about what should be on your signs. We've already talked about how you need to put up a sold sign once you've sold a property, but what goes on that sign before the sold sticker is slapped across it? It may not seem like the most important topic in the world, but if you look at the statistics, they'll show that the second and third most popular ways for buyers to find homes is with for sale signs. So, let's talk about what should be on your sign.

For starters, you obviously want the basics—your name, contact number, and picture. Please, have your picture on it. That is your branding. It is who you are. People will recognize you if you're showing the property or walking down the street. It coincides with all the other marketing and branding strategies that you're using.

I was attending a training event a while back as a trainer, and I noticed that one of the students didn't have their picture on their business card. There was another trainer who noticed this and thought, "Maybe this guy just doesn't have enough money for this. I'll give him some money to get business cards with pictures on it." So, he asked the student, "Why don't you have a picture on your business card? Is there something going on? Can you not afford it? What is it?"

The student replied, "I'm just so darn ugly."

And the trainer continued, "And what's your point?"

"Well, I don't really want people to see me because I'm ugly."

"Well, what are you going to do, surprise them with it? What's the difference? At least they know who you are. Put your picture on it. If you're ugly, pretty, whatever it is, at least they're prepared for it if you really are ugly."

It's the same thing with your sign. Your face is part of your brand. It doesn't matter if you're a supermodel or the homeliest person to ever walk this earth, your face is part of your business. The clients don't care what you look like as long as you can solve their problems.

I have gotten so much feedback through the years about my branding: "Brian, I see you everywhere."

The best part is, I don't actually have to be *everywhere*, just my face does. Clients see my picture on my signs, advertisements, newsletters, mailings, grocery carts, etc. One of my team members actually took a picture each time they saw a picture of me during a 24-hour period, and it was pretty profound; it really did seem like I was everywhere.

When people know what you look like, they feel more comfortable working with you because they feel like they know you. So, put a picture on your sign. I'm not talking about a *tiny* picture. Make your headshot as big as you can so people can clearly see who you are.

Once you've got the basics taken care of, you can figure out other items that can be or have to be on your sign. If you've got a good website, go ahead and put that on there. It most likely will not be a deal breaker to not have your website on your sign. But it doesn't hurt to have one other avenue for people to reach you or find out more about your business, even if it's not that good of a website. I put my website on my sign, and I've never had anyone say anything negative about it.

Some offices and brokers require you to put their office number on your sign as well. Now, it's obviously crucial that you follow all the rules set up by your brokerage and laws established in your state. But you can follow the rules and laws in place without hindering your own business, so make sure that the main number on the sign is your cell phone number. Bold it. Make it larger than the other numbers. Whatever you have to do to make sure the first number they call is yours.

Your sign is informational, but it is also another piece of your branding, so make sure you've got your picture and your other important business information on there. It's all part of your brand, so make your brand stand out.

Masterminds

"A mastermind alliance is built of two or more minds
working actively together in perfect harmony toward a
common definite object."

—Napoleon Hill

In Napoleon Hill's book, *Think and Grow Rich*, he talks about the importance of mastermind groups. But what is a mastermind group?

A mastermind group is simply a gathering of other professionals and individuals who have a common goal in mind, and that is to help each other grow each other's businesses. In a mastermind group, people will work together to support each other and help each other's businesses. Oftentimes, in a mastermind group, if you bring a challenge to the group, it's likely that someone in that group has encountered that challenge and may already have a solution for you. On the other hand, if someone else brings up a challenge, it may be something that you have already solved. In addition, should someone in the group bring up a strategy that they are considering, members of the group can work together to refine that strategy, evaluate it, and perhaps help that person determine if that strategy is likely to be successful. In truth, you can accomplish more in a very short period of time in a mastermind group than you might be able to accomplish in years without one.

Now, I'll give you my version of the mastermind group. It's basically a group of like-minded individuals working toward a common cause.

I've been a part of so many different mastermind groups, and I would highly recommend being a part of a real estate mastermind group. Regular high-minded, high-end mastermind groups are great, but make sure you belong to at least one *real estate* mastermind group.

How do you get into one of these groups? It's pretty simple. Just ask. Ask the people who you'd like to have in the group, and I would recommend you ask people who are doing WAY more than you're doing, the ones who are at the level you want to be at. Now, why would they want to be in a group with you? Simple: You are facilitating it, and you are running it. What's a better trade off than that? You're going to run a group, and these other individuals can collaborate and join together and share ideas. It's a fair trade of time and talents.

It is also ideal to be in a mastermind group composed of agents outside your market so you are not in competition with each other. When it comes to license law with this, if you're in the same state, you need to be careful about what certain information is shared. Most of my mastermind groups were across the country, so we didn't have any issues with that and were free to discuss any topics. We weren't afraid of competing with anybody directly, so it allowed us to be more open with each other.

A great way to find people for a mastermind group is to make connections within the training groups and other real estate organizations and boards you're a part of. Any time you attend events around the country, connect with the people there. Invite them into your mastermind group.

I usually do mastermind group meetings once a week in the morning. Some people do them every other week; some people do them once a month. It's really up to your preferences and the preferences and schedules of the other members of the group. There were times where I had a mastermind group meeting every single day for different parts of my life, not just for real estate.

So, if you're not in a mastermind group now, find one or build one yourself and reap the benefits of having a group of professionals there to support each other.

Professionals Need a Coach

There are two different types of coaching that I recommend. There's personal coaching where you deal with your personal life, and then there's professional coaching, which deals with your real estate career. I recommend you have both. Continually trying to stay in balance with your life is something that I think is crucial.

Now, when I say personal coaching, some people are going to think of counseling or therapy, which I'm also a big fan of. But the difference that I see in coaching versus counseling is that with counseling, I tend to feel like I'm just complaining for an hour at a time. With coaching, I feel like I spend more time talking about I need to do moving forward. What are the steps that I need to take? What do I need to do in the next week to get to where I really want to go? Personal coaching can help you make sure that your personal goals are moving forward and in the direction you want them to.

The same thing applies to business coaching, and if you don't have a real estate coach, please get one. Give me a call. Maybe we're a good fit and we can start our coaching relationship right away. Maybe we're not a great fit, but I can still help you out by setting you up with someone else who will probably be a better fit for you.

Why is professional coaching so important? Because these coaches have been there before. Why shouldn't you benefit from their experience? Why not take their advice? Why not take their direction on activities and referrals to other professionals? You can read a book all day long (believe me, I've done it over and over and over), but when when you can actually talk to someone and have them truly hone in on what you're missing or what you need to focus on, it can take your career forward very, very quickly.

About 15 years ago, when I first heard of somebody taking coaching for their real estate business, I was confused. "Why don't you just take a training course?" I didn't truly comprehend what it was all about. So, I get it—I get your hesitancy. But understand that when you get high enough in your business, there simply isn't the same amount of training available, and you're not likely to find training programs that give you the solutions you may be looking for at a higher level. Even if you're just getting started, some of that one-on-one coaching is crucial to help you avoid the pain that you're going to go through in the future. I personally like to avoid that pain right up front. And if coaching can help with that, all the better.

One of my coaching clients from New York, Clive (Clive the Client), was coaching with me and wanted to increase his real estate business. He'd been in the business a while and had found success in different ways but not anywhere near the level that he wanted. When he started with me, I could tell he was going in too many different directions, and I wanted to narrow his focus. I worked with him to narrow it down to the one thing he could do that would change his career and make him the most amount of money. After just over a few months, he was able to figure it out for himself as a part of the coaching process. Clive now knew where he had the most success and what he needed to do to increase that. He had the answers; he just wasn't asking the right questions. And that's what coaching can provide.

Now, I don't know the exact statistics of his success at the moment, but what I can tell you is that Clive feels so much better about his choice. The enjoyment of what he is doing has changed, and the time he is able to spend with his family has also changed. It's increased.

Sometimes, it's just finding that simple focus, that one direction, that one thing that can get you to where you want to go and eliminate the others. Coaches are there to guide you to that focus.

When you engage in coaching, masterminds, or in accountability, you have to recognize that you may encounter one idea that changes your entire trajectory. And there is power, there is a great strength in just one idea, and sometimes, one idea becomes priceless. When you place yourself in coaching or in masterminds, you set yourself up in a position to encounter those ideas that can be life-changing. So, if you don't have a coach, please get one. Check out the online coaching programs or contact me, and let a coach change your life like my coaches have changed mine.

*   *   *

Want to discuss putting the 52 Secrets to work for you? Schedule a complimentary consultation through my website at www.brianernstcoaching.com. I would love to discuss your options with you personally.

Accountability Partner

We've talked about being a part of a mastermind group, personal coaching, and professional coaching. Now, we're getting to accountability. Do you have an accountability partner? Do you have someone who helps keep you on track?

"Well, wait, Brian, how do we fit this all into a 20-hour work week?"

Don't worry. I'm not asking you to commit to a daily, hour-a-day conversation with an accountability partner. I'm talking about a quick, five-minute check in at most. Sometimes, it's even a text message. Just something to make sure you are doing your top five activities each day to work toward your goal. So, find somebody out there who you can help stay accountable and who is just as driven and focused to do this as you are.

It can be as simple as telling that person, "I'm going to make these phone calls today." Then, at the end of the day, check in with them to say, "This is what I did. This is what I didn't do." When you have that accountability partner and you share your progress with them each day, it helps you take care of tasks you didn't want to do and forces you to take the steps to do them. If you didn't get something done and weren't too afraid to tell your accountability partner that you didn't do it, maybe you just learned that it was a task that wasn't important and you can work on continuing to focus on those tasks that are important. Having an accountability partner doesn't just help keep you on track, but it can help shine a light on tasks or behaviors that are counterproductive to your goals.

Brian Ernst

If you have an accountability partner right now, that's great. Ask yourself if they help you move forward on the daily tasks that you need to get done. That's the main focus of the accountability partner: the daily tasks.

Now, if you have one that isn't working out very well and they forget to call or text, GET RID OF THAT ACCOUNTABILITY PARTNER NOW! Get a new one. I want you to be RUTHLESS about this. This is YOUR progress. What's it worth to YOU? This is all accountability. If they're not showing up, you need to find somebody new. You can just as easily forget to keep yourself on task; you don't need someone else to do it for you. Make sure your accountability partner is actually accountable.

Now, if you're not showing up, you have to address that too. Accountability partners only work if both parties are committed. Every day, whatever you agree to do, you should do that 100%. We're talking about five minutes a day here. It's not that big of an ask, and you shouldn't hesitate to ask it of yourself. No man is an island. Let someone help keep you on track; you'll both benefit and see the success that follows.

Consider this horse pull analogy by Jim Stovall:

"Draft horses... are very large, muscular animals that, throughout history, have been used for pulling great loads and moving very heavy objects. A single draft horse can pull a load up to 8,000 pounds. The strength involved in this is hard to imagine. So then we can speculate what would happen if we hooked up two draft horses to a load. If you instantly thought two draft horses could pull 16,000 pounds if one draft horse can pull 8,000 pounds, you would be wrong. Two draft horses pulling together cannot pull twice as much as one. They can actually pull three times as much. The two draft horses that can each pull 8,000 pounds alone can pull 24,000 pounds working together.

"The horses are teaching us a very clear lesson in teamwork, but they still have more to teach us. If the two horses that are pulling together have trained with one another and have worked together before, they can't just pull three times as much working together as they can by themselves. The two trained horses in tandem can

88

actually pull 32,000 pounds, which is a load four times as heavy as either of the horses could pull by themselves.

"The powerful lessons that these magnificent draft horses can teach us involves not only teamwork but coordinated and trained collaboration. No one lives or works alone as the proverbial island unto themselves."[1]

---

[1]   https://timmaurer.com/2012/01/16/horse-sense/

Consistent Prospecting

I've made a few observations of the real estate agents that I've coached and trained through the years. I see their production go up and down. They focus on lead generation and prospecting. They have business. They work on the business. Those deals close, and then they've got nothing. They have to start all over again. It's almost like an EKG; it just goes up and down.

So, there's a secret that I want to divulge right now, and you can't hear me, but I'm laughing as I think about because it really is just that obvious yet somehow still forgotten. It's consistent prospecting. You have to stick to your prospecting schedule. That is it.

For me, it comes down to marketing and making sure I am doing my marketing each month, whatever form it takes. When I'm doing my face-to-face interactions, I have that set in my schedule. I don't deviate from it at all. It's set in there, every single month, the same things. It HAS to be in place.

Now, for people who are going to do more lead generation through cold calling, for sale by owners, expireds, etc., you have to protect that time. That time is your WHOLE BUSINESS. Without that time, you're out of business. You might be thinking, "Well, that's not really a secret, Brian." Well, when I start to see more agents actually practicing consistent prospecting, then I'll believe you. Until then, this book will remind you since even veteran agents seem to need the reminder. The average agent out there does about six deals a year. Seriously. SIX DEALS A YEAR? There's no way they're doing consistent prospecting and only doing six deals a year. I honestly don't know how these agents keep their businesses running and are able to support themselves. Likely, they're not. The agents I have coached that have been in that category weren't surviving on their real estate business and had to make money with a second job. Please don't be in that category.

As a real estate agent, if you don't have a consistent, reliable, duplicatable way of bringing in new business, clients, or leads, you're not actually running a real estate business. You just have a hobby. If you're only doing real estate at the hobby level, you're likely going to end up with too much time on your hands that just ends up getting filled with busy work and activities to actually bring in business. Whatever form your prospecting takes, stick to it, and do not deviate from it whatsoever.

There is one agent I've worked with on and off, Betty (Betty the Bouncing Agent), who has been in real estate for probably as long as I have been in real estate. She's bounced around from different brokerages and training programs, but she has never been comfortable with prospecting in lead generation. She's never put a system in place to bring people in consistently, which means she's had to work other jobs throughout her entire real estate career. She called me a little while back to say she was going to drop out of my group even though she had just come back after a previous break from the group. She'd just decided that she no longer wanted to be in real estate any more. And you know what? That's okay!

I told her, "I think that's okay. I think that's great that you've come to that conclusion. I think for years, you've tortured yourself. This is the system that you've have never put into place, nor have you been comfortable doing it because you've never done it consistently. It's not a system that you've been able to duplicate, and it's definitely not been reliable. You don't want to do it, so it's smart to get out now.

Betty wants to help people, but she didn't feel like she was doing that with her real estate business. She's tried many different ways to get it to work for her, and in the end, it just wasn't for her, and that's okay. Real estate is not for everybody. She told me, "Brian, I can work anywhere for a couple of bucks. My cost of living is not exactly high, and I want to help people." She wants to do more work like helping at a women's shelter and doing other volunteer work. She continued, "I'll work whatever job just to pay the bills."

I said, "You know, that's great if that's what you enjoy and that's what you want to do. I think you should do that." I think that gave her a sense of relief from the guilt and shame and pressure she's put on herself for so many years, and I hope she gets what she wants out of that decision.

So, I know that's not the real estate success story you were expecting, but it is a lesson of what happens when you try year after year to build a business without creating the proper systems to be successful, especially without a consistent prospecting system in place. One of the tools I offer in my coaching programs is how to develop a viable, consistent prospecting system so you can be successful. If you need help with this today, check out my website and join my coaching program so I can help you develop a consistent prospecting method that is reliable and duplicatable.

*   *   *

Want to discuss putting the 52 Secrets to work for you?
Schedule a complimentary consultation through my website at
www.brianernstcoaching.com. I would love to discuss your
options with you personally.

Delegating

Do you delegate every part of the job you don't have to be directly involved with? This could be anything from setting up a sign to putting a lockbox on the property. Who does those activities for you? There are services and companies out there that exist just for those specific activities.

What I've done for most of my career is to find people who do just one part of the job and do it very well. I pay them a flat fee for their services and only use them if I actually have a listing for them to attend to. So, I don't have to hire a full-time staff to do activities like setting up lockboxes and signs that only happen occasionally.

Break down every part of your job. If you don't know exactly what you do, start on a Monday and write down the list of activities you do throughout the day. Then, at the end of the week, go through that list and organize it into the different facets of your job. Now that you've got your list, give it a thorough look and determine what activities you can hand off to somebody else. Then, look up the services you can sign up for to help take care of some of these tasks; focus on the ones that won't cost you more than it costs you to do the tasks yourself (remember what your time is worth!). Finally, sign up for them! You'll be amazed at how much more productive you'll be with the extra time you now have.

I can't tell you how much time I spent driving around, picking up signs, lockboxes, etc. When I finally made the choice to cut those activities out of my schedule, I gained back HOURS of time. I also have an attorney that handles the majority of my deals. Once the deal is under contract, I hand it to him. He takes care of the rest, including everything with the title company. Though every state is different, if you're in a state where you have to deal directly with the title company, you can have somebody set up who is ready to take over for you in that situation, leaving you free to move on to the next deal.

Too often, people spend time working on their current deals versus going to the next one. If you think about it, once you get into a deal, what's the likelihood that it is going to fall apart at that point? What percentage of your deals have fallen apart once you get to that stage? For me, it's a very small percentage, and I bet you have similar results. So, if you don't have to worry about the fate of that deal, where should your attention be? It should be on getting new deals under contract.

So, really give a hard look at all the tasks and activities your business requires because there are many different opportunities for delegation. If you're trying to condense your work week down to 20 hours, delegating various tasks is a great step in that direction. Delegate every part of your job that you don't have to be directly involved with, and you'll not only be happier but have much more time to focus on growing your business.

Secret 32

Take Care of Yourself

My experience in real estate is that most agents are available every waking hour of the day, seven days a week. Unfortunately, it often takes precedence over family time, personal time, and even work time if they're not focusing on their own business but helping or working with other people. What they're missing is the very important self-care aspect.

Taking care of yourself is one of the most important tasks in any industry and in life in general. It is hard to take care of others when you haven't taken care of yourself first. I have seen countless agents with health issues because they either work too hard or they don't feel like they deserve to have time off. These agents are the motivated ones who work hard and really want to succeed. But what they may not yet understand is that they won't be able to have long-term success if they run themselves into the ground.

You need to set boundaries and stick to them. When you're first ramping up for new business, I know it helps to be available seven days a week, but if you don't draw a line for when that constant availability ends, you'll run yourself ragged. Recently, I had a client who called me four times between 9 p.m. and 8 a.m. the next morning. He emailed me a half-dozen times, texted me I don't know how many times, and did the same thing to one of the agents on my team as well. It goes back to Secret 1 — there is no such thing as a Real Estate Emergency. Nine times out of ten, these issues get solved by the next morning, but because I kept seeing these notifications come in, it was disruptive because it got my mind spinning. I then had a hard time getting to sleep, which was my own fault. Normally, I turn my phone off in the evenings or once I start receiving messages because I know I'm my best after a good night's rest, some breakfast in my belly, and time to review all the new information. But I did not turn off my phone at any point on this particular night, and I suffered the consequences.

Another way to take care of yourself is to take care of your physical self. Do you go for weekly deep tissue massages? Do you work out on a regular basis, at least three or four days a week? Are you eating healthy?

I know you know these things, but are you actually doing them? In real estate, there's no one there to hold you accountable, and that can lead to some very bad lifestyle habits. Bad habits can then easily lead to other problems like addiction. It happened to me a little over a decade ago. I was addicted to painkillers, and it screwed me and my business up.

Accountability to yourself, your own personal health and sanity, is crucial. Make sure you have at least one day off, at a minimum, but take it off for yourself—not to get your oil changed, get your hair done or your nails done, whatever it may be. Make sure you're actually taking the day off and not just filling it with other work. I consider those things maintenance and not necessarily self-care in the same sense of renewing and recharging yourself. When you've got a full tank of gas emotionally, mentally, and physically, you can take on more difficult challenges and get through them with fewer battle scars and enough energy to tackle the next challenge when it comes.

Systems in Place

I've seen many agents' businesses grow, but I've also seen them fall apart. One of the fastest ways I've seen a real estate agent's team or individual business fall apart was due to the dependence on *people*. Now, I'm not saying don't have people in your life. I'm saying have *systems* in place.

People will come and go, but the systems are not really replaceable. I am not being ruthless. I'm just saying that people get sick, people don't show up for work, things happen. You can't have everything riding on one person then have to stand by and watch it all crumble when life happens to that person. Instead, have systems in place so that you're a systems-oriented, not people-oriented, business. I would recommend you check out the book *The E-Myth* by Micheal E. Gerber. It talks about creating an operations manual that documents every piece of your business. If you have a system in place for each part of the process in your real estate transaction and you lose a particular person for whatever reason, you can find somebody else to do that particular system. You can hand the new person the manual, and they can jump right into their business responsibilities.

When you have it spelled out exactly what needs to be done, you don't have to lose weeks, months, even years, to get back up again because of the loss of *one* person. I once had a courier who was primarily in charge of picking up signs or lockboxes for me, but then he let me know he was moving. So, I put together a list of exactly what he did and put it out there to find somebody else to replace him. It wasn't a long interview process, and I was able to continue to do business as usual as the new person took over the tasks of the one I lost.

One of the horror stories that I've witnessed was an agent who lost their licensed assistant. This assistant did most of this agent's business for her, but they ended up parting ways after a while, and it collapsed the agent's business. That can be really scary.

Don't get me wrong, I am not advocating for *not* growing your team or your business. Actually, I'm a big proponent of that. But I *am* here to remind you that you need to have the systems in place so you're prepared if anybody steps away from their job for whatever reason. This is crucial for your business' long-term success. So, if you don't have systems in place at the moment, make it happen NOW.

Task Management

Are you familiar with time management? I'm sure you've heard the phrase, and it sounds like a simple enough concept. But when you really think about it, can you actually control time? If you're Doc Brown from the movie *Back to the Future*, maybe you can. But I haven't met him yet, and I'm guessing you haven't either. So, really, what you need to focus on is *task* management. Focus on identifying what tasks you can do in a specific amount of time. Time will keep on going. But you *can* control what you do *within* that time. It's just a change to how you think about your day. Sometimes, people think it's just semantics, but a simple word change really does change the meaning of the phrase. So, focus on *task* management and see what a difference it will make in your business.

One way to manage your tasks and maximize your time is by scheduling and time blocking. When I first got into the business, I was taught to take your week-at-a-glance calendar (mine is digital) and block out your tasks in order of importance. Mine gets blocked out in this order:

God
Family
Everything else

With real estate, you *do* have enough time. If you block out two hours here, an hour here, three hours there for family, and a client can't get ahold of you during that time, you're merely on an appointment. It's just an appointment with your family. Blocking out your time like this makes it not only doable but easy to track your time and ensure you're only working 20 hours or less a week!

God
Family
Everything else

I recommend time blocking EVERYTHING. This is the task management part. When do you get up? When you go to bed? When do you eat?

To be honest with you, there have been times in my career when I've forgotten important items on a regular basis. People would ask me, "Brian, how'd you lose so much weight?" Well, it's really simple. You work. You work some more. You go to bed. Then you get up and you do it all over again. Nowhere in there was designated time for lunch or dinner. That's what I don't want YOU to go through. It's not a healthy weight loss regimen. This is where it's really important to have balance in your life.

With the time blocking method, you basically take the effort to block off 20 hours a week for what you're ACTUALLY GOING TO DO. You put it in that timeframe because the other hours of your week are focused on what's really important to you. So, use whatever method works for you. I personally recommend time blocking, but whatever you do, make sure you're using your time effectively and practice task management to do so.

Give Yourself a Raise

Now we get to one of my favorite subjects: making more money and giving yourself a raise. Would you like a raise? There's one easy step to do it. Are you ready? Raise your commission!

"Oh, no, Brian. I can't do that because of the competition, and..."

I don't want to hear it. Just raise your commission and thank me later.

I can't tell you how many times I've gone on a listing presentation where the seller was interviewing other people who quoted commission rates lower than mine—1%, 2%, 3%, even 4% lower than my commission—but I still ended up listing the house!

Just because someone charges less money doesn't mean that is who the seller will pick. They're looking at your *value proposition*; they want to know if you can alleviate their concerns. Can you solve the seller's problems? People will pay a lot of money if you can truly solve their problems. Think of it that way. If what you offer is the answer to their problems, they'll gladly pay extra.

You might still be skeptical, thinking, "Well, that might work for you, Brian, but it probably won't work for me." So, let me tell you about another agent that is a part of my coaching program. Uma (Uma the Underconfident) didn't charge a high commission because she didn't think she was worth the extra commission. After some coaching, she was able to see her true value and worth; she examined what her time was worth and all the expertise she brought to the table. Once she felt comfortable with it, she gave herself a raise and quoted a full percentage higher on the next two listing appointments she went on. And it worked!

The higher percentage didn't scare the sellers off, and they were happy with the service she provided. Long term, Uma now has more money as a direct result of the higher commission, and her confidence is higher, making her an even better agent and an overall happier person.

Let's break down the numbers if you still need some convincing. A 1% raise in commission is not a 1% raise in income and gross profit, but it's actually 1% percent raise on commission, which could actually be anywhere from a 15% to 20% increase in income. The raise and commission doesn't raise any of your other expenses; instead, you're raising your revenue, and it's simply extra money. Break it down! If you're splitting that commission with another agent, it could be as high as a 30% to even 35% percent increase in income just by charging that 1% difference, depending on what commission rate you are at. So this raise you give yourself is HUGE.

I see so many agents lower their commission just because someone asks them to, and they don't realize what a huge percentage of their income they're giving up. Unfortunately, when you break it down to expenses, for most real estate agents, they're giving up their profit by doing that. Because of all their other fees that are involved, including their expenses, their marketing, etc., that 1% change in commission could make a difference in what they actually net from the commission. For some agents, that means they're no longer making any money. Some think they can make up for a lower commission with volume, but it just doesn't work that way. If you're giving up profit on one deal and you multiply that by 100 deals, you're still giving up profit on each of those, and the deficit is never made up.

Even if it isn't about the money for you, when you decide to lower your commission for one or 10 clients, you're setting a precedent that you're willing to concede to their demands, which changes the power dynamics in the relationship. When the client thinks you'll give into their every demand, the deals take longer, so even if you wanted to increase your income by doing more deals, you no longer have the time to do so. You're offering them a service that comes with your time and your expertise. How can I, as a real estate agent, be expected to protect my clients' financial interests if I can't even protect my own commission? How can I be expected to protect one of their biggest investments if I can't protect my own investment in myself, my business?

So, protect your business and have confidence in the value of your work and what you provide to the client. Go ahead and raise your commission. That's it. Raise your commission. Whatever you're charging, go 1% higher. You won't regret it. Give yourself that raise now.

*   *   *

Want to discuss putting the 52 Secrets to work for you? Schedule a complimentary consultation through my website at www.brianernstcoaching.com. I would love to discuss your options with you personally.

Don't Give Up Your Commission

Hopefully, by now, you're clear on what my views are on commission. But if you're not, I'll give you a little more insight.

I was in a training course maybe 15 years ago that was taught by a RE/MAX broker owner. Her main message was, in every part of the deal, throw in your money. Throw in your commission. Get through the deal. It's only 500 bucks here, it's only 1,000 bucks there. Whatever it is, just get through the deal. She was advocating to give up your commission whenever possible. I might not be being fair—it wasn't *exactly* her message, but that's how it came across to me. So, I started to do that. A couple hundred bucks here and there, and then it became more like a couple thousand bucks here and there. At one point, I asked myself, why the heck was I doing this? It wasn't helping my business any, so why was I continuing to do it? I decided at that point to draw a line in the sand and never cut my commission.

So, now, that's what I do. I NEVER cut my commission, and I NEVER give up my commission during a deal. If I'm listing a home and somebody says, "Well, you take this for a commission," I just say no and stick to my game plan.

You'd better have at least three commission-handling techniques off the top of your head for every given situation you're going to get in. If you don't know any, why don't you give me a call? I'm happy to teach you because it is SO crucial.

Never cut your commission, because it sets a precedence. People talk. When I started raising my commission, it was kind of tough because my clients knew my commission at a certain percentage, and when I changed it, they felt like they were being taken advantage of.

When you're consistent across the board, *that* is what's fair. So, when you're in a deal, in negotiations with a home inspection, whatever it may be, keep it consistent. Often, my clients turn to me and say, "Oh, Brian, throw in your commission." I'm not a party to this deal. I don't get to engage people in that conversation, and I tend to just avoid it. I show them their choices instead.

"What would you like to do?" "Here are your options." Not one of those options is throwing my commission into it. Because what happens is if that deal falls apart, you're going to give it up on the next deal too. Are you going to do two deals and give up the money? That doesn't make any sense.

So, keep it as a general rule not to cut your commission and not to give it up in any part of the deal. When you get to the closing table and somebody wants to play hardball and says, "Well, I'm not going to sign unless somebody gives up a thousand bucks," don't give in. There are many different parties at that table. Don't be the one who speaks up. That's why I don't even go to closings; that way, I can ensure it doesn't turn on me.

Please, make it a rule that you never cut your commission and you never give up your commission, ever. It will make you more money in the long run and save you time and hassle.

Don't Disclose Your Commission

Never tell anyone your commission unless these four requirements are met:

They are sold on you.
They are sold on your company/team.
They are sold on the price.
They are sold on the timing.

Often, when someone asks me what my commission is, I haven't even seen the property yet, so I simply respond, "I don't know, I haven't seen your home yet. Let's get together."

Those four factors need to be in place before you give up any information. If those four things are not put in place, you DON'T TELL ANYBODY your commission. Why? Well, it's very simple. You're not going to list the property.

If you don't know what the price is, if it isn't in a timeframe you think you can feasibly complete the deal in, if they clients are not really sold on you, what are you doing there? It's irrelevant. Your commission is nothing because you're not going to list the property.

Don't share your commission with anybody. It's nobody else's business. It's your business. If you're going to share it with somebody, you need to make sure they're sold on you, your company, the price, and the timing.

One of the agents on my team was doing an open house. She ended up in a conversation with a potential seller in which she shared her commission with her. She thought they had made a connection, and so she shared the information with her. I was less optimistic because, based on my experience, if you don't have all four of the items I mentioned earlier—you, your company, price, and timing—the potential seller isn't invested enough and already sold on you and the company to go for that commission, whatever it is. And that was the case again, in this instance. The potential seller never called her or got ahold of the office.

I can't tell you how many times I have been in that situation or seen that situation over the course of my career. I'm now very careful not to share my commission before the four conditions are met, and I don't even share my commission at the beginning of the listing appointment because I don't look at their house right away. I want to make sure I have the right information; **until the value they see in you is higher than your commission**, it doesn't make any difference. If you haven't shown them how you can solve their problems, why would they pay you any commission if they don't know you can do it?

You'll get some pushback, for sure. Potential sellers want quick answers to their questions: What is your standard commission? What is my home worth? But if you explain that to better serve them, you can't give them accurate answers until you've met with them, seen the property, and fully evaluated the situation, they'll respect you for that. Because even though they want the fast answer, they also don't want to be taken advantage of, and they want good service.

I respond to persistent inquiries with, "I don't know what I'm selling yet. I run a real estate business, and until I know what I'm selling, for what price, and under what timeframe, I don't know how much it's going to cost you. Let's get together, and let's figure it out. I'm happy to share that with you when we get together and I have seen your home."

Often, people will forget that you're running a business. A real estate agent isn't the same as a sales clerk in a department store who will tell you the price of the item before you decide if you want it and either buy it or not. But in real estate, there are many more factors. If I'm not going to list your property, my commission is zero. If you want to overprice a property and not take the time to fix it up based on my recommendations, I'm going to charge a higher percentage because I know it will take longer to sell the property. It's not a simple answer, so I insist on having more information before I give it.

Until you have all the information you need, until all four requirements have been met, set up an appointment and wait until you *do* have all the information. Don't just disclose your commission before *you* are ready and you are sure the client is going to be truly receptive to it. Just don't do it.

*   *   *

If you would like to schedule a complimentary consultation, please visit my website at www.brianernstcoaching.com.

Secret 38

Intervals

All right, so we have talked about time blocking and scheduling, and this next secret falls right in line with those ideas. Re-engineer intervals. Every quarter, I put an appointment on my calendar to re-engineer intervals. I know that sounds like I could be introducing a new-age fitness trend or engineering project only an MIT grad could complete, but this is a simple task that you can and should be doing regularly. Re-engineering your intervals involves reviewing everything I had in place over the past three months, including any mailings, marketing materials, advertisements, contacts I've made, and appointments that I had. I assess the past three months and see if I need to make adjustments for the next three months.

If the marketing materials I put out there don't seem to work (and they don't always work right away), I have to evaluate it and figure out if it's something that still has potential or if I should ditch it for the next quarter. I don't want to be hyper-reactive, so I take this time to fully evaluate the system and make sure there's been enough time to truly evaluate its effectiveness. Sometimes, I don't know after three months, so I wait and evaluate it again another three months later.

If I were you, I would open your calendar right now and put an appointment on the first day of the quarter, for every quarter, to re-engineer intervals. I would block out at least an hour of your time to assess your numbers, what you've done in that quarter, and any adjustments that need to be made. It's not complicated, but it is an important task that needs to be done quarterly to ensure continued success.

Branding

Branding is a huge topic, and for the longest time I really didn't even consider it, but I was actually doing it. I spent 14 years of my career with RE/MAX, and I was branding myself to RE/MAX with the RE/MAX balloon. That was my branding. It was already in place. You just put the picture in, and the rest was taken care of. I didn't have to worry about anything on my signs; I just worked with the existing templates. It's a very simple and easy concept to get if you don't actually have to think about it.

But if you're not working with a brokerage that has branding in place or you're working for yourself, you do have to take some time to consider your own branding. So, whatever company you're with, you're branding your face, your name, and your company, which all needs to tie together, as well as the colors and the combinations. It should stay consistent across the different platforms. You should have your picture on your signs (you should know to do that by this point in the book) as well as on your business cards, and it should be the same picture. Your car, your website, etc.—it should all match.

I've seen some agents who have completely different profiles for different marketing sources, and it's hard to connect their different marketing strategies when they don't even look the same. If someone sees your ad online and on a park bench but they don't match, you'll be less memorable. That's two different faces or or two different logos they have to remember instead of remembering the same face or logo twice.

So, what is your defining piece of branding? Is it your picture? Is it a logo? Whatever it is, keep it consistent. You want people to remember you, and you don't want your marketing to blend in with all the other content out there.

I don't want to give you all the research and present a dissertation on why it's important to keep your marketing simple, but I do want to help you see long-term results with your marketing. And if you make your branding consistent over all platforms, you will have much more success with your marketing strategy.

Book Your Vacation

Out of all the secrets I've shared, this is going to be the most fun and also the most difficult. I know it was for me. Going on trips and booking vacations forces you to change your systems. If you're not available, who is going to handle your business? How is it going to be handled? I spent several years where I was actually traveling on the road for a variety of reasons, and it added up to about three months each year. That helped to shape my business and refine how to do this all on a 20-hour work week.

So, what I'd recommend is deciding where you want to go take a vacation with your family, with your friends, or going solo. Where do you want to go? GO BOOK THAT TRIP. If you've been in real estate for a couple of days or a couple of years, you might realize that a lot of business seems to happen the day or so before you go on vacation. That likely won't change, so just embrace it. Plan for how you're going to handle it.

Are you going to work on your vacation? I mean, that kind of sounds nuts, and I'd done it for years, so I think it's nuts. When you go on an actual vacation, you're NOT ANSWERING YOUR PHONE. You're actually *enjoying* your vacation. A vacation is your opportunity to have other people step up and handle your business. I hate to burst your bubble, but you're not the only person who can do what you do. I know it's a hard concept for some people to grasp, but other people have been real estate agents before, and there will be other real estate agents in the future.

So, go ahead and enjoy yourself. Go make a mess out of your business. Now, I don't mean that you should purposely mess up your business, but planning a vacation provides you with the opportunities to rise to new challenges. The world, and this business especially, isn't static, so you need to be comfortable tackling whatever comes your way. New problems will always come up, and if you don't plan to take at least a week off, let's just say every quarter, you'll burn out.

Even if you're out of town for a training event, do you want to be checking your voicemails, text messages, or emails every five seconds? Or do you want to really be present where you're at? You'll only get the most out of a training event if you're fully present in it. If you're splitting your attention between the event and your phone, you won't give quality attention to either, and you'll be shortchanging yourself and your business.

So, go set up a vacation RIGHT NOW. Go do it, book it, and set up who is going to handle the business. Just taking the time to set up the systems in preparation for your absence will dramatically change your business. A lot of what needs to be taken care of consists of day-to-day activities, and it doesn't hurt to help get those streamlined at any point. Go plan your trip, and enjoy that vacation spot that you've been putting off visiting. Your future self says, "Thank you!"

I'll Call You

I like to call this secret the "Don't Call Me, I'll Call YOU" secret. It's really about setting expectations. When you're trying to condense your work week into 20 hours, every phone call you have with your clients is crucial because some clients can take more time and have more concerns or more needs than others. On each of those phone calls, I set the expectations and let them know what will happen next and who will reach out to them.

I tell them, "You don't need to call me; we'll call you when it's time for the next step." If you don't do this and set expectations right from the start, clients get panic-driven because they don't know what's going on. They build up a variety of scenarios in their head that have no basis in reality. They haven't gone through this process a million times like you have, so they freak out.

By the time they actually share that information with you, they're already freaked out. If you don't even pick up your phone or you're not available, they freak out even more. This is where setting the expectations come in. That's why you need to let them know upfront what will happen. You let them know that you *will* call them with any information when you have it and that they should not need to worry about calling you. Also, let them know your work hours. Tell them you won't even have your phone on during your off hours.

You should say, "I'm going to contact you next," or, "This person's going to contact you next."

It's a very simple. Before you get off each phone call with each client, tell them when you're going to be communicating with them next.

Now, what I've done for years is I specifically call sellers on one day, buyers on another day and block out the time on my calendar. I do this one day a week just to check in with them, even if I have nothing to tell them. I just say, "Hey, just want to check in with you. I have nothing to share with you." So often, seller complaints are about the lack of communication with their agents. With this technique, when you set up those specific expectations before you get off that call each time, you drastically diminish the number of phone calls you get from your clients.

I could be carrying 30, 40, 50 listings at a time, and my phone ISN'T EVEN RINGING. How cool is that? Well, actually, my phone is ringing, but those calls are from prospective clients—not the clients I am currently working with. But really, it isn't coming in from the current clients, complaining about something or asking questions. So, set those expectations and think of it this way: Don't call me, I'll call you.

Secret 42

The Right Market

Identify, market to, and work with the right clients. That's it. Work with the right clients. Now, how do you actually do that? That's a little more complex.

If you're going to build a geographic farm where you plan to send mailings, do open houses, and go door-knocking, make sure you do your homework. That means figuring out who's the dominant agent in the area and what marketing he or she is doing. How many homes have sold, and is there enough turnover? What's the turnover rate, and does it make sense to even market in that neighborhood? What's the market time in that neighborhood? There are many factors that go into play when choosing a geographic farm. So, make sure you do your homework so you can increase your chances of success.

The other part of marketing is your friends, your family, your book of business, the sphere of influence, etc. These people are sources that will send you business. Think about who those people are. If you're going to be in real estate for a couple years (I originally thought I was only to do it for a few years; I had no idea where this was going, and it's now been 16 years!), your relationships make a significant impact. Figure out who those people are. Figure out who will send you the most business, who *know, like,* and *trust* you and who will refer you and recommend you to their friends.

It takes a while to develop this, but once you do, that's your database. I can pretty much guarantee the majority of agents don't have this setup. When those agents complain about not having enough business, it's because that part of their businesses were not set up right, and they are not targeting the right people to work with. Those right clients will make your job easier.

I actually had a past client reach out to me because he wanted help buying his next house. He moved out of state, but he had such a great experience with me that he wanted to work with me again. At this point, I had a whole team set up, so it was such an easy handoff to them. He knew and trusted me, so he was more than appreciative for the referral to my team. In the end, we got him what he was looking for. Another successful interaction with this client.

It takes a while to build the right database, but think of it this way: You should enjoy the people who you're working with, and if you don't, maybe you don't have the right database in place. That's really a point that I want to drive home because at the end of the day, if we did everything *solely* for money, we'd live our lives differently. You might as well enjoy it.

The Breakup

Identify and end bad client relationships quickly. How do you do that? How do you identify a bad client relationship? For me, it's really simple. If they take three, four, or five times the amount of time, money, effort, or energy out of me than my average client, I know they've got to go. Think about the number of deals can I do in that amount of time if I took that one person out of the equation!

I see it all too often. If I have a seller who messes up a deal when we have a solid deal, they are going to be a pain in the butt. Are we going to do this again, and again, and again? Do they really want to sell? We have a buyer who puts offer after offer in, a low-ball offer here, a low-ball offer there. I don't usually like to use the word low-ball, but basically, do they keep putting in unrealistic offers that I know the seller probably won't take? When you can identify bad client relationships, when you realize these people are realistically never going to buy or sell within a realistic timeframe, end it.

It goes back to identifying this relationship from the beginning. Were they the right people to work with? Did you ask enough questions in the beginning to properly identify if they would be a good client? I know their motivation. I know why they need to move. I know when they need to move. I know all the details. So, I should be able to make a sound decision.

In a situation where someone's relocating to another state and they have to sell their house before they buy the next house, there's usually a stronger motivation in there. When you have a client who doesn't *have* to move, doesn't really *want* to move, and you feel like you're talking them into something, the motivation is lacking, and they'll likely take up more of your time than you may want. That's usually how I identify a bad relationship, based on the amount of time I'm spending. If I'm spending too much time on them, taking too many phone calls over and over and over, and fielding too many emails and text messages, I'm wasting my time. If I'm spending more time with one client than I am with all the rest of my clients, I'm not in a good relationship.

When you discover that you're in that type of situation, part ways as amicably as possible and as soon as possible. Maybe you can hand it off to somebody else as a referral, still get paid on it, and let someone else spin their wheels with them for the next six months. That way, you still make money, *and* it saves you time, money, and energy.

Speaking of energy, how much energy did that person drain from you? When you talk to someone who really trusts and respects what you have to say but you just don't have the energy for that person because the problematic client zapped it out of you, it's simply not fair to them or you. It's not fair to the client who really appreciates what you have. So, end those bad client relationships quickly.

One of my coaching clients, Lisa (Lisa the Likeable Agent), took on a listing at a very inexpensive commission. She took it for 1%, though she could have gotten three times the commission on her side. However, she didn't ask for that much because the seller convinced her to take the 1%. The seller had been fired by a previous real estate agent and was known to be very uncooperative and obnoxious. On top of all of that, the seller wanted more money for her place than her place was worth, and the comparable property she was using had a 50-year age difference to her property. But Lisa went along with it and listed it at the price the seller wanted.

Lisa also found out that the seller was actually getting kicked out of their condominium by the association. Do you know how hard it is to get kicked out of a condominium association? I mean, I've closed over a thousand deals, and this was the first time I ever heard of someone being kicked out like that. I know it happens, but I had never actually seen it. What did this person do? I have no idea, but it's a HUGE red flag. And if that wasn't a big enough red flag, it also came out that the seller was in a lawsuit with the condominium association. So, at this point, the red flags are raised, and the sirens are blaring. Don't do business with this client!

I would identify Lisa's client relationship as one I would have never gotten into. Surprisingly, Lisa actually knew most of the client's faults in the beginning. She called me about it after she had already listed it. I told her, "I believe you need to part ways with this person as quickly as possible," and then gave her the instructions on how to do that legally so she wouldn't get into any trouble.

But, unfortunately, she did not take my advice. Lisa called me later and she said, "Brian, I am having heart palpitations because this client is driving me crazy. I am worried about my physical health." When it gets to the point that your physical health is in jeopardy because of a client you took on, you need to end that relationship right away. Putting your health on the line for your job like that is just nuts.

The bigger issue here is the fact that Lisa could have helped so many more clients if she wasn't wasting her time on the problem client. I feel like it's an elementary school equation: How many more clients would Lisa have helped in the amount of time she spent distracted with this one seller? Keep in mind that she wasn't on the phone with the seller all day long. They were short conversations here and there, but it consumed her mind so much that she could not focus on anything else. That's crazy!

When she finally did get rid of the client, she was a whole different person. Imagine that. Identifying a bad client and a bad client relationship and ending it quickly can make you more money. When you are in that kind of relationship, you are not necessarily thinking logically; you are just thinking of the craziness you are involved with, and that doesn't help anybody.

We've all been in a situation in which we're hungry for new clients and we're tempted to take on those clients that we know are going to be incredibly challenging. But you have to try and keep in mind that taking on one bad client will not only make it a challenge for you in completing the deal and earning your commission, but it will probably also take away from other commissions that you would otherwise be able to earn. You will be so busy trying to babysit this one problem client that you will fail to perform prospecting and other tasks necessary to bring in great clients. So, the moral of the story is this: Choose your clients wisely and be willing to break up with a client if it gets bad.

Dress for Success

When I got into sales right out of college, I felt like I wasn't enough. Now, that was my own personal issue, but regardless of where the issue stemmed from, I used my outward appearance to compensate for that feeling. I always dressed for success. I then carried that right into real estate.

I like to dress at least one level up from what my clients are wearing. In general, I wear a suit and tie to every listing appointment and for every client interaction that I have. It's an image I put out there. I made this super simple for myself by only wearing white dress shirts. When I have to go to an appointment, I don't have to pick what color dress shirt to wear, and every tie matches. It's pretty simple.

I have dark-colored suits. I have solid-colored ties. I don't have to think about it, and it takes one more step out of the whole equation that saves me time. I essentially have a uniform, and honestly, it's worked so well for me. It coincides with my branding, this image that I market out there of myself, and it all lines up when people actually meet me. "Wow, you look like your picture!" That's the idea! Sometimes, I even tell them that, depending on the situation.

So, do you dress for success? What that looks like will be different for everyone. Whether you're more into style and fashion and want your clothing to reflect that, or you want something more simple and standard, either way, make sure you look like you care and your look matches your branding. Dress better than everybody else in the room. Whatever works best for you, keep it that way. And don't think about it too much—it saves you time.

Headsets

This might be one of the simplest secrets I have. Use a headset. I found that I can accomplish so much more with a headset than without. You might be thinking, "Oh my gosh, this is what you're telling me, Brian? Not exactly breaking news!"

Well, let me get into a little more detail on this. I use a headset that plugs into both of my ears, so when I'm actually talking to a client, I can hear them so much more clearly. I am really focused in on that conversation versus how I would be if I were holding the phone up to my head. If I need to be on the computer while I'm on that phone call with that client, I can take care of that immediately. I can and do also take care of other things. If I have to throw in a load of laundry or some other household task, I'm able to do that *while* on the phone, which saves me time. Throwing a load of laundry into the machine is not exactly rocket science, so I can still be 100% mentally focused on the phone call.

Now, the quality of your headset is crucial. If your client can't hear you, you've wasted that time on the phone with them. They may have misinterpreted or misheard you, which can cost you money and a lot of headache. So, I do go through a lot of headsets, but it's worth it. I'd recommend one that incorporates both your ears, so that you can be totally focused in on the call. If anybody ever tells you that your voice isn't coming in clearly, check your headset. If you can't fix it, go get a new one. I usually have several headsets at home, ready to switch out at a moment's notice. Make sure you're working with a quality piece of equipment, and increase your productivity and focus with a good headset.

The Eight Criteria

Don't go on a listing appointment unless these eight criteria are met. In fact, I wouldn't even consider it a listing appointment if they aren't. I've wasted too many appointments in my career not having these met upfront. With these eight criteria met upfront, you have a much higher chance, a better conversion rate, for turning that into actually getting a signed listing agreement. Now, we can talk about what not to do before you go on a buyer's appointment, but if you've been paying attention to each secret to get you to this point, you should know that you're not going to bother with going on a buyer's appointment at all. For this program to work, you're not working with buyers. So, BEFORE you go on an appointment, get the sellers on the phone and gather all of this information.

1) **Do you know your clients want to sell?** However you want to get it out of them, do you know that this seller actually wants to sell? What's their motivation? Why are they moving? You will need to find out at what price the clients would like to list their home. So, it's critical to gather as much information as you can on this subject.

2) The second thing is to make sure you have enough information about the property to do a **ballpark market analysis**. I'm a big advocate of a one-stop, one-step listing appointment. Make sure you're prepared.

3) The third criteria, and this is something that is a challenge, is to **find out how much your clients want to sell their place for**. I'm going to tell you this: Often, people will not answer that question, or they'll give you a response of, "That's why we have you coming over." But you want to know how much they'd like for their place, so you have to be persistent. Now, don't keep asking the same question over and over again; that's how you annoy and possibly lose clients. Instead, try asking the same question again in a few different ways. For example, you can ask, "How much have you seen similar homes in your neighborhood going for?" If they answer with a certain number, they'll usually add some commentary like, "But I think it's way overpriced," or, "I think they could have gotten more." Now we're getting somewhere. You can continue that conversation to find out more about what they're looking for. I want to be as prepared as I can to go into that listing appointment and show them that they might want to rethink their original number.

4) The fourth thing you want to do is **qualify them over the phone**. Can they actually sell? What do they owe on the place? When the market crashed, I can't tell you how many times I had people who owed way more money than their home was worth, and that wasn't including any of the fees for selling their property. Now, that doesn't mean I dismissed the appointment just for that reason, but I made sure there weren't going to be any surprises when I did start down that path with them. I looked at other streams of money they might have and made sure they would be able to actually sell the house and still pay any outstanding fees.

5) The next step is confirming that **all the decision-makers will be present**. Now, that's not just a husband and wife who were on a title. I'm talking about their parents, kids, and anyone else who is involved in the decision. Often, I'll have people request to have certain family members there. Great! Let's get them all together. Or, can we get them on the phone? Can we get them on a video call? What can we do to make sure all the decision-makers are present and that we don't have to do all of this again in a week when Aunt Suzy gets back into town?

6) The next step is making sure you **schedule enough time** to go through everything you want to go through. I generally schedule about two hours with people, and if that's an issue or a surprise to them, it gives me some insight, and I usually try to dig deeper to find out more. Either they're not that serious about this, or they may have other agents coming in. So, I ask, "Who else are you speaking to about selling your home?" It's kind of an open-ended question. It's not the most pertinent question in the beginning of the process, but some people will just say, "Oh, I'm talking to my parents about this," or, "I'm talking to my kids about this." Okay, great. Sometimes, they say, "Oh, we're looking at these three agents." Okay, now I know a bit more about what's going on. The more information I can get, the better.

7) **Find out what objections there are to overcome?** Here is a question to ask the sellers: "If you like everything you see and hear and the price feels right, would there be anything preventing you from getting your home on the market?" Isolate the objection by asking if that is the ONLY thing preventing them from moving forward when we get together. If not, we keep asking the question until we determine ALL of their objections. The purpose of this is to be prepared for the listing appointment with all of the documentation or anything you can show them to overcome their objection AT THE LISTING APPOINTMENT. We are not trying to overcome all of their objections over the phone. It's better to have the time to prepare and have these conversations face to face.

8) The last step is **sending your pre-appointment package to the clients**. Years ago, that was an actual physical binder that I would get to the clients ahead of time so they could look at everything that I had to offer, including my marketing plan, and then, I'd pick it up from them at the appointment. Today, what I do is send them an electronic marketing plan. I confirm that they received it and that they have had a chance to take a look at it before I actually go on the appointment. I want to do as little selling of me at the appointment as possible. Obviously, there's still some of that, but I want to make sure they're pre-sold on me before I walk in the door.

If you can accomplish all eight of these tasks and abide by the criteria before you go into a listing appointment, your conversion rate will be much higher. You'll waste a heck of a lot less time in the process, which then means you'll achieve more money in less time.

* * *

Want to discuss putting the 52 Secrets to work for you? Schedule a complimentary consultation through my website at www.brianernstcoaching.com. I would love to discuss your options with you personally.

Have a Backup

Picture this: A new real estate agent is starting to rack up some expenses just by being in real estate; they have a couple deals under their belt, and right now, they have one deal that's under contract. That one deal will pay for their mortgage payment, the car payment, insurance payment, etc. Now, imagine this: That deal goes sideways. How would *you* feel in that particular situation?

I've been there. I've done that too many times. It's awful. You hold your breath waiting on an appraisal to go through. You hold your breath during negotiations on a home inspection or on their financing going through. The secret is this: You need to have so many deals that you can afford to lose one. But even further, you need to have so many deals that you could afford to do a deal for free each year.

If you raise your commission, you should be able to afford this. Now, why would I want to do a deal for free? Well, there will be situations that come up where you really want to help somebody and they just don't have the money to sell their house. Maybe you want to help out somebody close to you, or you're helping out a friend of a friend you owe. Maybe it's just out of charitable contribution; whatever it is, you want to be in a position to be able to make it happen.

If you don't have enough deals right now that you can afford to lose one, well... my advice to you is pretty simple. GET MORE DEALS! If I go back through the years that I've been in real estate, I've probably done at least one or two deals each year for free. It's a great feeling to have that freedom. Make sure you have enough deals that you're not holding your breath as you wait for a deal to go through, and you are able to help someone if the situation arises.

Private Listings

Are you familiar with private listings? Not everybody is, and you'll often hear a range of different terminology for it. Sometimes, people use the term pocket listings. Quite personally, I find that phrase offensive. Somebody's biggest financial purchase or investment is something you're putting in your pocket? I don't like that kind of implication. I call them private listings, and what I mean by private listing is a property that isn't on the market right now but will be during a certain timeframe.

These listings come from sellers who are not quite ready to sell today, but they are planning to sell in the future, and they want to sell in a specific period of time—when school gets out, at the end of the year, during a transition at work, etc. It's a way to confirm you're getting the listing ahead of time; you might even be able to sell it ahead of time as well and get your seller what they want.

"So, with private listings, I'm able to list the property today in the private network, but I don't put it out on the multiple listing service (MLS) as an active property for sale until my clients are ready." I've done this for years, and I've taught other people to do it as well, really changing the course of their businesses in just a few months. Now, how did I do that with them? I encouraged them to start building their inventory in December, January, and February instead of waiting until the spring to actually get the listings on the market. Being able to get a few more listings going during those months that are usually a little less active can really impact your business for the better.

If I can get you the money you want for your place and close in your timeframe, would you list your house today? When I ask the sellers this question, I'm trying to alleviate the two major objections that I usually get to private listings. That way, right off the bat, they can start to have faith that I will solve all of their problems. I let them know that if they have any other objections, I can work with them on those as well and help make the selling process as stress-free as I can. "I can get you the money you want; I can close when you want to close, and I'm not gonna advertise it like crazy until you're ready." I'm simply stating facts while also combatting any objections they may have so I can get them to sign the paperwork *today*.

In years past, I would just keep the start date open on the contract, and they wouldn't know much different. Now, I have a rider on my contract that basically states that the property is not to be placed on the multiple listing services until a certain date or until given notice by the seller. It's that easy to incorporate into your current business.

If the seller is sold on a price and on the timing, why am I not moving forward with these people? Why am I waiting three or four months? I want the sign in the yard today!

Why not? That's the big question. Ask it of yourself: Why not? It adds to my inventory, adds to my sign presence, and it develops a whole other market for me. What do I have to lose? Ask it of your seller: Why not? If I have a buyer who will wait six months to close on this place, if I can get it sold when and how you want it but save you the stress of having to worry about it actually happening, what do you have to lose?

A few years back, I was in one of my mastermind groups, and I shared with a fellow agent how I do private listings. At first, he was very skeptical about the concept. The challenge he was having was that most people needed to take some time to get their homes ready and prepared for the market. His listing-appointment-to-listing-taken conversion ratio wasn't as high as I think he'd like it to be, and we were directly addressing that conversion rate. So, I asked him why he wasn't getting the listings, and he responded, "Well, they needed to fix their places up."

"Okay," I started, "but why didn't you list it right then and there? Then, you put it on the market when they're ready. It's called a private listing." I continued to explain to him how he could make it work with the contract by postdating or leaving the start date blank, and I mentioned the other benefits and facets of private listings. When I ran into him later, he told me that in the first three or four months that year, he had taken more listings than he did in the past two years, just because of private listings. His initial skepticism turned into surprise success.

Just as it made a huge difference in his business, private listings can make a huge difference in yours as well. We just had a three-month period recently in which I was selling a private listing every single week before it hit the market. Recently, there was a three month period where a private listing of ours sold every single week BEFORE it hit the public market. Another just sold the other day; it was put on the private listing network on Friday and had three offers by the end of the weekend. It wasn't ready to sell yet, but it was still a multiple-offer situation! This seller said, "We don't even know if we can actually move until Monday because of our job situations." But now, they have some options if they are able to move, and they don't have the stress of having to worry that their house won't sell!

I come across so many sellers who don't even realize this is an option, and when they do, it opens up a whole realm of possibilities for them. I list quite a few properties generally in the same area, so when one property goes under contract, I usually have people who are interested who didn't get that property. And it's great, because I can then contact the agents and say, "I got this coming up; would your clients be interested in this?" They're happy because they didn't have to go hunting for a new property, and I'm happy because I've got another deal in the works.

It's a win-win situation that I have incorporated into my business. At any given time, I have at least one private listing in the works. So, try it out! It's fun, and you get the satisfaction of actually fulfilling the needs of your clients right away.

Secret 49

Your Support Team

All the secrets I've shared with you so far, if put in practice together, will transform your business. BUT if you don't have your support team at home, it's going to be hard to keep this all in place. Now, what is your support team at home? It's your family and your friends. Do you go off to work each day, and your kids say, "Hey, Mommy, Daddy, when am I going to see you? Will I see you tonight? Will I see you this weekend?" That can really hurt; those questions will get you straight in the gut. But if your family feels supported because you are able to spend time with them and you make it a priority to turn off your phone and take vacations, they will be much more likely to support you. Imagine, instead of wondering if they'll see you, the kids say, "Hey, Mommy, Daddy, you know, I hope you get that listing. I hope you get another sale today." That can make your day so much better, just those words of encouragement.

Do you have family goals? Have you sat down with your family and shared goals that you want to accomplish as a family? Learn what everybody wants, and together, create vision boards. I have quite a few vision boards, but having that family vision board with a pictorial representation of what we're trying to achieve as a family or individually is huge for my family and me. It will be for yours as well.

Now, how do you track this? I would suggest a goal thermometer. You put it on the pantry or closet door (anywhere works fine as long as it is somewhere where you and your family will see it every single day). Then, as a family, you have to determine how you'll accomplish the goals and what the reward will be if you get to a certain level on the thermometer. Let's just say the family wants a trip to Hawaii. What needs to happen for you to be able to take your family to Hawaii? List out what needs to happen, then track it.

Whatever the goal is, break it down and put it into a goal thermometer. Make a big poster of that for everybody to see. When you all work together toward a common goal, each member of the family is brought closer to each other. You all support each other because you are all working toward the same goal. So, make sure you have a strong support system, and work hard to keep it.

*   *   *

If you would like to schedule a complimentary consultation, please visit my website at www.brianernstcoaching.com.

Write It Down

With all the new ideas that you're putting into place, it is so crucial that you write everything down. I don't mean literally put everything down on paper, but you should somehow document everything. I keep a to-do list with me on my phone so I can continually reference it throughout the day. I hate to miss one thing, one negotiation, one call back that I need to make to get another deal, so I make sure each important item is documented somewhere so I don't forget it.

Take notes, even if they're small or a random ideas that comes to you in the shower. Write them all down because they may come into play later. If you are making handwritten notes, take the time to type them up later so you don't have to worry about losing that piece of paper and can keep all your information in one place that's easily accessible. Then, later, review the notes. I'll review them each week and will sometimes even go through them all again at the end of the month.

I review the note or comment and ask myself, "Is this something that I want to put into place? Is it an idea for something else?" Then, I make tasks or set up calendar appointments from the actionable items. Each day, I go through the to-do list, and at the end of the day, any task or calendar appointment that wasn't a priority or didn't get done gets moved to the not-to-do list. The next day, that list helps form the to-do list, and if, at the end of the week, it still hasn't been done, I figure it wasn't important, and I clear the list out at the start of the new week. I can always go back to an item, and I can always pull them back up. But it clears my calendar, clears my list of things to do, and clears my mind.

Brian Ernst

Since doing this, I've never forgotten anything, and I can always refer back to a note or comment if I need it down the line. I make sure everything is dated so I know when I came up with a certain idea or know when I told a client something. Make sure you write everything down; it will help keep your life and your business more organized.

Don't Be Everything

My last secret is this: Don't be everything to everyone. JUST BE A REAL ESTATE AGENT. Unfortunately, with real estate agents, it has become the norm to do activities that don't necessarily get you paid, thinking that you have to know everybody, do everything, and have connections for everything. You don't. All you need to do is be a real estate agent.

I don't usually have connections for everything, like different plumbers, electricians, those types of things, off the top of my head. It's a great practice to have, but if those people screw up, it's your reputation. I only recommend a few people in a real estate transaction who I know and trust will get through it and handle the problems.

Too often, I see real estate agents feeling obligated to do things that don't make them any money. For example, in my area, it's customary when the buyer's agent has completed a contract that they get that earnest money to the listing agent or the listing agent's office. Now, does that mean that that buyer's agent has to physically go do that? At the end of the day, the check just needs to get to the listing agent. If you just give the instructions to your client and explain how it works, you can save yourself the trip. It's perfectly legal for them to do it.

I'm not trying to say that you should do this to manipulate your clients or anything like that. I'm just saying they *can* probably get the check to the agent faster. It saves your time, *and* it makes them happy because they confirm they have the deal.

With every step you take in a real estate transaction, think about whether or not you will make money by doing it. If you're doing something as a real estate agent, question it. Why do we do it this way?

Brian Ernst

Do we have to do it this way? If it's not a license law or a board rule that you have to follow, why are you doing it? I would question yourself on all your activities. Don't be everything to everybody. Just be a real estate agent, and have fun with it!

The Ultimate Secret

The ultimate secret is not one of the secrets you've already read. In fact, I just told you the previous secret was the last one, so what's this ultimate secret all about? The ultimate secret is is putting all of the other secrets together: The COMBINATION is the secret. All these ideas put together! These secrets are all things that I have learned throughout my career, through other programs, trainings, real estate and business transactions, and personal growth. And I wouldn't be at this point in my career without putting all of that knowledge together to succeed. If you don't have the right combination of ideas, you don't have the right COMBINATION to open the safe. The secret is the COMBINATION, and the COMBINATION is all the secrets combined to get you to this point.

Five years ago, I got into a relationship with someone who lived out of state, and I wanted to spend time with her, to travel to her. We were both in real estate, and we both did real estate trainings and training events. I had a goal of reaching the $250,000 mark, but it was hard travelling all the time and spending an average of three months out of the year away from my home. I had already created a program that was all about making $250,000 on a 20-hour work week, but I wasn't hitting that 250 mark. My goal wasn't big enough; I missed that one piece of the combination. Because I didn't have the whole combination, I wasn't successful. So, I doubled down on the secrets, and I embraced the travelling I was doing and increased my goals.

That's how this program turned into *The 52 Secrets to Making a Half Million Dollars a Year While Working a 20-hour Work Week*. When you only have a limited amount of time, let me tell you, you bust your rear to get something done! I would only have a certain number of days at home, so I made the most out of them. I would schedule appointments back to back to back, which meant that I *had* to be efficient; otherwise, I wouldn't be ready. I was motivated to get the work done and be successful doing it. I prepped people as much as possible. I confirmed the appointments, reconfirmed, made sure I had my homework done for each one, and then, I went out there, and I listed a lot of properties. And I sold a lot of properties because I didn't have the time not to.

I think many people have other priorities that take them away from work, but they still want to be successful in their businesses; they just don't want to lose their lives outside of work. That's where I was; I wanted something bigger, and I wanted something different for my life. So, I adjusted how I approached the business, I used these secrets *together*, and I found success. You can too! Don't short-change yourself or go along with what society or other outside influences are telling you to do. Take a chance on yourself, and start the transformation of your business today. Go to my website now and sign up for the online course. Your business will benefit, and your personal life will benefit. You only get to live this life once, so make the most of it. Don't wait. Start your new life today!

Conclusion

I want to thank you for reading this book. I really appreciate the time and dedication you put forth to read from Secret 1 to 52. I've spent my whole career figuring these things out and putting the combination of secrets together so I could share them with you. I'm happy I could do that, and I'm excited to see what you do next with the information.

How do you implement all these ideas, these secrets, this transformational information in combination together? I'd recommend focusing on implementing one secret a week. In a 12-month period, if you've accomplished all of these goals and incorporated them your business and your habits, you'll be a completely different real estate agent. You'll have a completely different real estate business.

In the meantime, I wish you the best of luck with your business and all you hope to accomplish. I appreciate you reading this, and if I can help at any point along this journey, please don't hesitate to reach out to me. Enjoy the start of your business transformation!

Interested in putting the 52 Secrets to work for you?
Schedule a complimentary consultation through my website at
www.brianernstcoaching.com. I would love to discuss your
options with you personally.

May I Ask a Favor?

Hey, it's Brian Ernst here, and I'm the book's author.

I hope you've enjoyed the book, finding it both useful and fun. **I have a favor to ask you. Would you consider giving it a rating on Amazon, please?** My ambitious goal is for this book to be considered "a coaching classic," and one way to help establish the book's status is with a boat-load of Amazon love that speaks to why its valued.

Many thanks in advance,

Brian Ernst

About the Author

Brian Ernst has over 16 years of real estate experience, making him one of the top-producing agents in Illinois. As CEO of the Brian Ernst Realty Group, he successfully manages a $30+ million-a-year production team. Brian uses state-of-the-art systems and best-in-class processes that ensure his clients get what they want and need. Utilizing his real estate expertise, Brian is also a motivational speaker, group coach, mastermind facilitator, and a consultant.

Brian believes in the importance of being in a constant state of learning and developing professionally. His ability to apply his growth mindset has translated into outstanding results for his clients. Brian has managed and coached agents nationally to achieve up to a 400% improvement to their businesses. He also presents hundreds of free workshops to help any individuals who want to accelerate their success.

Brian attended Indiana University, Western Illinois University, and Benedictine University for business management and MBA studies.

Brian Ernst can be reached at: **https://www.brianernst.net/**

Printed in the USA
CPSIA information can be obtained
at www.ICGtesting.com
LVHW021642220923
758689LV00024B/150/J